Furnace of Renewal

A Vision for the Church

George Mallone

InterVarsity Press
Downers Grove
Illinois 60515

InterVarsity Press is the book-publishing division of Inter-Varsity Christian Fellowship, a student movement active on campus at hundreds of universities, colleges and schools of nursing. For information about local and regional activities, write IVCF, 233 Langdon St., Madison, WI 53703.

Distributed in Canada through InterVarsity Press, 1875 Leslie St., Unit 10, Don Mills, Ontario M3B 2M5, Canada.

Acknowledgment is made to the following for permission to reprint copyrighted material:

From the Revised Standard Version of the Bible, copyrighted 1946, 1952, © 1971, 1973. All quotations from the Scripture are from the Revised Standard Version unless otherwise noted.

From the lyrics to "Fifty Ways to Leave Your Lover," © 1975 Paul Simon. Used by permission.

From "God's Warning, God's Remedy" by Kevin and Dorothy Ranaghan. Originally published in New Covenant, P.O. Box 8617, Ann Arbor, MI 48107. Used by permission.

Cover photograph: Robert McKendrick

ISBN 0-87784-605-7

Printed in the United States of America

Library of Congress Cataloging in Publication Data

Mallone, George, 1944-
  Furnace of renewal.

  Includes bibliographical references.
  1. Church renewal.   2. Christianity–20th
century.   3. Bible.   O.T. Malachi–Criticism,
interpretation, etc.   I. Title.
BV600.2.M343   269   81-15669
ISBN 0-87784-605-7   AACR2

17	16	15	14	13	12	11	10	9	8	7	6	5	4	3	2	1
95	94	93	92	91	90	89	88	87	86	85	84	83	82	81		

Dedication

*To Bob Birch
who encouraged my fainting spirit
to dream of a
renewed church*

Foreword

In 1982 one may rightly ask, "Why another book on church renewal?" The answer should not be long in coming, "Because the church is still unrenewed." But have we not spent most of the last decade talking about and reflecting on the renewal of the church? And have there not been conferences and seminars *ad infinitum* addressing the question? Indeed, have the Christian media not created their own new class of guru, the church renewal specialist, who now commands the highest fee for a speech and to whom is accorded the accolade "most relevant" in our generation?

Yes, all of this is true, but the fact remains: the church is not yet renewed! That is not to say that we are lacking showers of refreshment, or that individual churches are not experiencing blessing, or even that some of the traditionally "dead" churches are not seeing new life. We may be thankful that this is indeed happening. And the result is in no small part a response to, as well as the creator of, the hunger evidenced in the rise of spokesmen for and books about renewal.

There are many aspects to renewal, even as there are many different people God has used to begin renewal in his church. There is liturgical renewal, there is the rediscovery of the laity, there is the recovery of the Bible and its message, there is the awakening consciousness of Christian spirituality, there is the revival of evangelical scholarship, and there is even a sign that the unhappy separation between theology and social concern is diminishing. All of this is evidence that God is alive in his church, and by no means limiting his activity to any single denomination, tradition or geographical center.

For George Mallone, and those of us privileged to share with him in the Christian community where he serves as a teaching elder, renewal must encompass all these elements and more. Our pilgrimage has been an imperfect and partial one, but in it we have discovered that God has yet more light to shed on his Word, and that the truth revealed from Scripture has a dynamic influence, through the working of the Holy Spirit, to change us gradually into the body he wants us to become. That we are not there yet is evident to any who observe us; that we are making halting steps in that direction is equally obvious.

I mention this background, for as you read what follows, it will be readily apparent that what George has written is not an abstract treatise on renewal, but the fruit of his study of one neglected book of the Old Testament, applied in the context of an unfinished but growing local body of believers, and watered by the refreshing streams of the Holy Spirit's ministry to the group. George has a unique way of relating all of this in book form, and it is my belief that Malachi's message will come to life for many through his book. But the real secret of the book will not be found within its pages; it will be worked out in other churches, some quite unlike ours, which by the grace of God begin to hear his Word and experience his Spirit in a new way.

Carl E. Armerding, Ph.D.
Principal
Regent College
Vancouver, BC

Preface

Five days after my conversion and halfway through my first church service as a new Christian, I discovered my spiritual gift—discontentment. Though the people were kind and the Bible teaching was edifying, I immediately sensed that there was something wrong with the church. Since I had no particular biases against the church, I assumed that these promptings were from the Holy Spirit and were to be used constructively for Christ's body.

All young Christians, I suppose, have their instant solutions for the maladies of the church. For most it is simply add water and stir. However, to those in control such advice is seen as conceptually crude, childish or unworkable. The young Christian is told, "Go grow up; and when you do, you can sit on one of the boards." This reception has caused many to make an exit stage right from the church.

For a while I was one of those angry young Christians. I believed that God's real activity was on the individual level in vital, personal relationships with Jesus Christ. His presence was also found in small group Bible studies or in personal evangelism, sponsored usually by a parachurch organization. These covert activities always seemed to raise the dander of the church, but who really cared? In my own thinking, ecclesiology—the doctrine of the church—had no relationship at all with soteriology—the doctrine of salvation. I was about to abandon the institutional church altogether when I stumbled across a few books which looked forward to renewal in the church.[1] There was nothing wrong with the New Testament teaching on the church, said these authors. The problem was that the church was not fulfilling its mandate. There was evidence, however, that God was beginning to work in local churches with the same dynamic evident in parachurch movements. Although I still had no theological conviction about the church, I now had a desire to discover its place in Scripture.

Today, almost two decades after recognizing my gift, I am still fervently employing it. The difference is that I am now a critical lover, rather than just a critic. I have chosen to move into the glass house and live there with the others. I am thus more cautious about the stones which I throw at the church. I love the local expressions of Christ's body, and I would do nothing to see them destroyed. The church and the gospel are intricately related to one another, and any tearing down of one leads to the tearing down of the other. As St. Cyprian (Bishop of Carthage, A.D. 248-258) said, "A man cannot have God as his Father who does not have the Church as his mother."[2] At the same time, I feel no constraint or insincerity in pointing out some of the deficiencies I see in the church today, or, in the words of Albert Camus, to point out where the "soap is lacking."

English essayist and critic John Ruskin (1819-1900) once noted that "all books are divisible into two classes: the books of the hour and the books of all times." My heart's desire is that this book will be at least a book of the hour.

I owe more than can be expressed to those who have worked with me in this first venture. The elders and congregations of Marineview Chapel and Emmanuel Christian Community have provided most of my seed thoughts and working environments. My gratitude to them is immeasurable. Dr. Orby Butcher, my cousin, was willing to risk a little advance money, and my good wife Bonnie encouraged me through every depressed and lethargic period. My fellow worker Paul Stevens and Dr. Charles Hummel were kind enough to read the original draft and to make helpful suggestions. Mr. James Hoover of InterVarsity Press graciously and tenderly pruned my overgrown garden into something readable. Appreciation is due finally to Ruth Cuddeford, Janis Croft, Nancy Nichols and Mary Bingham for their faithfulness in typing and retyping my countless drafts.

They
Want
to See
Jesus

1

Several years ago my wife and I took a midnight flight out of Los Angeles. Once the wheels were secured under the belly of the plane, I noticed that the moon looked bright red. A southern Californian called it their "harvest moon," but to my wife and me, who live with the clear skies and coastal breezes of the Northwest, it was pollution.

Environmental pollution damages our health, but it also obstructs the beauty of God's creation. It keeps us from seeing the majesty of a sunset or tasting the refreshment of a crystal stream. The glory of God's character that he intends to reveal through his creation is marred and polluted.

So it is with another type of pollution—pollution in the church. In John 12:20-21, certain Greeks who had come to the Passover feast in Jerusalem asked the disciples for an audience with Jesus. "Sir, we wish to see Jesus." They wanted to meet Jesus in person. Discontent with only hearing about him or seeing him from a distance, they wanted to get to know Jesus more intimately.

Today many people are like these Greek visitors. They

want to get to know the authentic Jesus. And Jesus is available to them through his body, not in the fashion of Charles Templeton's novel *Act of God,* where the bones of Jesus are found in the basement of a Toronto apartment, but through his people.[1] He is incarnate, by his Spirit, in the church which is his body (Eph 1:22-23; 4:11-16; 5:23, 29-30).

Jesus declared in his high priestly prayer that he had given his glory to the church (Jn 17:22). His glory is the visible manifestation of his splendor and power. The Apostle John says that no man can see God now, for Jesus has returned to the invisible Father, but if we love one another we will have the assurance that God is in our midst (1 Jn 4:12). Paul, in his letter to the Ephesian Christians, assures them that the multifaceted wisdom of God is made known to the world by the church (Eph 3:10). The God who has so clearly revealed himself through creation (Ps 19:1-6), his Word (Ps 19:7-14) and the Incarnation of his Son (Heb 1:1-14), today by the aid of his Spirit reveals himself through the church.

But just as the smog distorted my view of the moon in California, so pollution within the church keeps people from seeing God's Son. They are hindered from seeing his full radiance and glory.

What Problem?

A popular psychologist was the speaker at a pastors' conference. As he introduced himself to each pastor, he said, "I'm sorry to hear about the problem in your church." Nearly half of the pastors responded, "It was there before I came." The other half said, "It is improving." However, one fellow responded, "What problem?" After playing golf with this pastor later on, the psychologist discovered he also lied about his golf score.

Every church has problems. The church without problems is a church without people. Arid experiences, relational frustrations and structural inadequacies are common everywhere.

For those who have endured such irritants, it is important to remember that these inadequacies affect not only us, but also onlooking non-Christians. They are far more aware of our shortcomings than we would give them credit. One bad experience, along with a dose of the electronic church on television, may be all that a thoughtful non-Christian needs to write the church off as hopelessly irrelevant and ineffective.

My own efforts in evangelism have convinced me that people do not generally reject the gospel because they are turned off by Jesus or by scientific arguments against the existence of God, or even by the moral standards demanded of a follower of Christ. Over and over I have heard people confess that their chief stumbling block to becoming a Christian is the church.

Revive Us Again
If pollution within the church so cripples its impact on the world, what are we to do about it? Spending more on media blitzes and personality spectaculars will not help the church grow nor rightly influence our culture. Howard Snyder, in *The Community of the King*, agrees, suggesting that church growth is not so much dependent on successful techniques as on simply letting the church be the church. "Church growth is not a matter of bringing to the Church that which is necessary for growth, for if Christ is there, the seeds of growth are already present. Rather, church growth is a matter of removing the hindrances to growth. The Church will naturally grow if not limited by unbiblical barriers."[2]

To remove the hindrances we must concentrate on renewing the church. "If the church wants to be a credible herald, witness, demonstrator and messenger in the service of the reign of God," says Hans Küng, "then it must constantly repeat the message of Jesus—not primarily to the world, to others, but to itself. . . . Its credibility—and no amount of energetic and busy activity can replace that vital factor—depends on its remaining faithful to the message of Jesus."[3] Non-Christians are "word resistant" to the gospel of Jesus Christ because they have seen little demonstration of that word. Therefore, as David Watson says in *I Believe in the Church,* "Unless renewal precedes evangelism, the credibility gap between what the church preaches and what the church is will be too wide to be bridged. It is only when the world sees the living body of Christ on earth that it will be in anyway convinced of the reality and relevance of Christ Himself."[4]

Revival and renewal are terms which are often used of the refreshing process so desperately needed in the church. Although there is debate over the definition of these words, in simple terms *revival* is an unconditional outpouring of God's grace which brings repentance in the people of God and conversion to non-Christians.[5] Some historians suggest that prayer is an integral part of the revival process. *Renewal,* on the other hand, is a revitalization of God's people so that they set themselves to obey his word (Neh 8; Hag 1:12-15).

I have witnessed both revival and renewal. Several years ago I was in one city where nearly fifteen thousand high-school students were converted in a four-month period. I call that revival. I have also seen churches come to grips with their biblical calling. Given time, proper feeding and healthy leadership these churches grew out of their institutional bondages and anemic walk. That was renewal.

A church may give its full attention to prayer for revival. But as it does it may overlook obvious needs in its own community. As Jim Elliot once wrote to his fiancée, "Let not our longings slay our appetites for living."[6] This aptly applies to our concern for revival in the church. We are to do the work of renewal and pray that God will in his own sovereign disposition send revival to the church. Our concern is to be faithful in obeying what God has already revealed.

A well-known Anglican charismatic, being interviewed once on a secular radio station, was introduced by his host as a man who was intimately "involved in the cosmetic renewal of the church." Regrettably, this slip of the tongue describes the attitude of many Christians toward renewal.

Genuine renewal of the church will not just touch up its fading image or repair a few minor cracks. Instead, the church must be refined in the furnace of renewal. Here, melted by the intense heat of God's love until all its impurities are consumed, the church can be made "fit to meet this hour."

Before we move on, it may help if I sketch where we are going. My own thoughts about renewal have taken shape largely around the book of Malachi. The state of God's people in his day, it seems to me, was remarkably similar to our own. So in the next chapter we will take a look at Malachi to see the message he brought from God. In chapters three through nine we will take up the contemporary implications of what we see in chapter two, looking at congregational worship, the sacraments, church leadership, divorce, tithing and covetousness. Finally, in chapters ten and eleven we will discuss the work of the Holy Spirit in giving power and in refining the church. Apart from the Spirit's work no renewal can take place.

In no sense do I want renewal to sound trendy, superficial or easy. It is not. As Charles Swindoll has said in the context of remodeling a home, renewal "will take longer than you planned, cost more than you figured, be messier than you anticipated, and require greater determination than you expected."[7] Evaluation and change are disruptive for the church, but they are God's constructive means for our growth and thus the way in which the world will be able to see the undistorted face of Jesus Christ.

God
Always
Says It
with Love

2

Charlie Brown's cut-rate psychiatrist Lucy gave this helpful analysis one day: "Discouraged again, Charlie Brown? You know what your trouble is? The whole trouble with you is that you're you!"

"Well, what in the world can I do about it?" replied Charlie Brown.

"I don't pretend to be able to give advice, I merely point out the trouble."

From the last chapter you may have concluded that all I wanted to do was to "point out the trouble." But I do plan to make some corrective suggestions for the church. Before I do, however, I want to make a detour in order to take a look at an oft-overlooked postexilic prophet, Malachi.

Strangely enough, as I suggested in the last chapter, we will discover in this fifth-century B.C. prophet to Israel a message for the church today. Malachi will point out to us four major areas of pollution in the church and the corrective measures which God desires us to take. In his message to Israel, Malachi denounced the contamination of worship, the tarnished nature of leadership, the befoulment of divorce and the covetous practices which robbed God of his due.

The church today can benefit as it listens in on God's word to Israel. Seeing these contaminants, God desires to disinfect his people, to "purify the sons of Levi and refine them like gold and silver, till they present right offerings to the LORD" (Mal 3:3). His intention is to refine a people to glorify himself, so that his name will be great among all the nations (Mal 1:11, 14). It was his intention for Israel; it is his intention for the church.

To see Malachi in his chronological setting look at chart A. This chart highlights over five hundred years of Israel's history. In 930 B.C. Israel's united monarchy split. No longer was there a single successor to the line of David and Solomon. Jeroboam, son of the Ephraimite Nebat, took possession of the throne of the northern kingdom (Israel). Rehoboam, Solomon's son, reigned over the southern kingdom (Judah).

Israel survived on its own for nearly two hundred years before being taken captive by the Assyrians in 722 B.C. The prophets Amos and Hosea witnessed to Israel's corruption and apostasy, yet repentance did not come. Judah maintained its independence for almost another one hundred and fifty years before they were taken captive by the Babylonians in 586 B.C. The pre-exilic prophets Isaiah, Micah, Naham, Habakkuk, Zephaniah, Obadiah and Jeremiah brought witness to Judah before its enslavement.

During the Babylonian captivity, two prophets are known to have written—Ezekiel and Daniel. In 538 B.C. Cyrus, king of the ruling Persians, issued a decree that allowed Jews to return to Jerusalem. In 536 B.C. Zerubbabel, the governor, and Jeshua (or Joshua), the high priest, returned to Jerusalem with the first group of expatriates. At that point God sent the prophets Haggai, Zechariah and Malachi to minister to his people. Though the Israelites

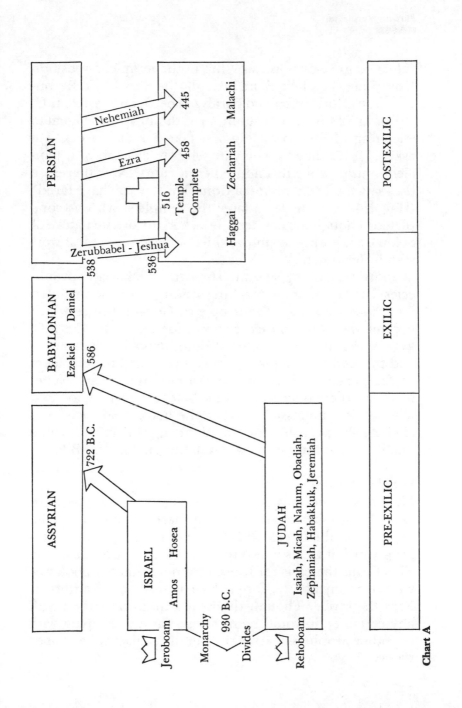

Chart A

returned to re-establish worship in the temple, opposition from Samaritan neighbors brought them to a halt. Reconstruction efforts remained paralyzed between 534-520 B.C.

But in 520 B.C. God summoned the prophet Haggai to encourage Israel to once again take up their work. He asked, "Is it a time for you yourselves to dwell in your paneled houses, while this house lies in ruins? Now therefore thus says the LORD of hosts: Consider how you have fared" (Hag 1:4-5). Four years later the temple work was completed. Though the new temple lacked the ornate nature of Solomon's, it once again provided a place for central worship in Jerusalem.

Shortly after Haggai's ministry came Zechariah's prophecies. In a series of far-reaching visions, Zechariah painted a glorious future for the people of God—a future which became the hope and expectation for Israel. In 458 B.C. Ezra returned to Jerusalem with another group of captives, and thirteen years later Nehemiah returned to Jerusalem as the Persian-appointed governor of Jerusalem. Nehemiah was there only a short time before returning to Susa. Though it is impossible to date the book of Malachi precisely, it was probably composed during the time of Nehemiah's visit to Susa, somewhere between 445-420 B.C.

Sunrise, Sunset
Malachi's name means "my messenger." This may have been the prophet's actual name or merely a title. When the Septuagint (the Greek Old Testament) translates this Hebrew word, it treats it as a title and not as a proper name. This forms the basis for those who hold that the book was written anonymously. Others have identified the author as Ezra the scribe. Though the issue cannot be settled with any certainty, it would seem natural and in keeping with the other prophets of Israel to identify Malachi as a proper name.

The latter part of the fifth century B.C. was a significant time in the Mediterranean world. This was Greece's golden age, the time of Pericles, Euripides, Herodotos, Xenophon and Sophocles. It was also a time when the Greeks began to celebrate victories over the Persian armies.

But if you had traveled two days by ship from Greece to Palestine, you would have found a much more sedate culture. Israel was then living in an uneventful waiting period. The nation was marked by poverty, foreign domination and near despair. They had endured over two hundred years of captivity under foreign lords. Since returning to the land their military might was low. They lived in tents ill-protected from the rains, and their farm lands were not producing because of severe drought. The temple had been rebuilt, but there was no glory attached to it. Religious duties were carried on without much enthusiasm or conviction. The spirit of worship had been lost in formal ritual. Externally they were worshiping, but internally they were apathetic.

Zerubbabel the governor and Jeshua the high priest had died. These men had held genetic links to the kingly priest line of the expected Messiah. Zechariah had brought hope that the day of prophetic fulfillment and of messianic deliverance was drawing near. But still under foreign governments and with no vital faith, Israel began to languish. Where was the kingdom of God? Where was the promised deliverance? Day after day the cynicism grew. There was a sense that one ought to give up; serving God was of no use at all. Despair led to agnostic cries, "It is vain to serve God. What is the good of our keeping his charge or of walking as in mourning before the LORD of hosts?" (Mal 3:14).

The period of despair was also a period of moral laxity. As Friedrich Keil has said, "The outward or grosser kind of idolatry had been rendered thoroughly distasteful to the people by the sufferings of the exile; and its place was taken by the more refined idolatry of dead works righteousness, and in trust in outward fulfillment of the letter of the divine commands, without any deeper confession of sin or penitential humiliation under the word of God."[1] It is refined idolatry that Malachi must address. His is the last word God will give his people for over four hundred years. It is a word that will need to sustain them during the period of the intense persecution under the Greeks and the long-fought Maccabean wars. It will be the last word until God's messenger Elijah (4:4) arrives in the form of John the Baptist. It is an important word for Israel to hear, and it is an equally important word for a morally lax and lethargic church to hear. A short summary of Malachi's message will set the stage for the chapters which follow.

How Have You Loved Us? (Mal 1:2-5)

What first comes to your mind when you know that someone is about to correct you? As a teaching elder in a Christian community, I have a number of people who correct me from time to time. Usually it is a correction I need. But my vocation does not make me immune to natural insecurities about correction. I want to know, Do they love me? Do they accept me? Do they have my best interests at heart? If they do, then I am confident that I can take any message they might give.

Likewise my wife and I learned long ago that a frontal assault in a marital spat never made the impact we desired. It only got everyone emotionally uptight. However, a word of assuring, faithful love was the best lubricant for administering correction. Malachi begins the same way, " 'I have loved you,' says the LORD" (1:2). No other Old Testament book begins with such a direct revelation of God's intimate care. These opening words teach us much about the nature of our God. He is not a frustrated drill sergeant who is always barking orders. He is not an anxious mother, always demanding perfection without ever assuring us that we are loved. God, when he speaks to us, always speaks in the indicative before moving to the imperative. Simply stated, God always speaks to us in terms of his forgiveness, power, acceptance, help and love before he ever makes demands of us.

Legalistic Christianity always emphasizes what we must do for God. But true Christianity, which flows out of grace, emphasizes that our obedience is a response to God's initiative (Rom 2:4). Obedience is not just response to his commandments, but response to his love, grace and forgiveness. These things above all else motivate us.

God's assurance of his love comes intimately. Malachi does not say, "The Lord told me to tell you he loves you." Rather in the style of the superintended prophet, he speaks to them in the first person, "I have loved you." The Lord is present in his words. They are an extension of his being. Though they come through Malachi's lips, they are still the Lord's words. The very form of the prophecy takes it out of the realm of speculation and allows the hearers to know that God speaks directly to them.

Have you seen the poster which says, "Smile, God loves you, and after all you've put him through that's really something"? Israel from the time of the decline of the monarchy put God through a great deal. They tried his infinite patience. Yet he remained loyal to his promises. But notice the skepticism with which this word is received, "How hast thou loved us?" (1:2).

Joyce Baldwin suggests that "the atrophy of human love in the community . . . has undermined confidence in the divine love, and there is no appreciation of the providential overruling of God which has made possible the return to Jerusalem and the rebuilding of the temple."[2] Since they did not see God's love in their relationships with one another, it was impossible for them to see God ministering love directly to them. I think if I had been God I would have said, "If you don't know, then I won't tell you!" But God knows that we often need evidence for our faith. We need a sure footing outside our own individual experience, an objective signpost on which we can hang our mental convictions. In and of themselves they are not able to save us, but they are able to point us in the direction of faith.

To show his people that this intimate expression of love was more than just an emotional liver-shiver, God reminded them of the twins Esau and Jacob. By natural right, Esau as the elder should have been the principal heir and recipient of his father's blessing. Yet God chose to love Jacob. To this thorny problem Baldwin suggests that "the Old Testament nowhere teaches that Jacob was more lovable than Esau, or more pleasing to God than Esau, though it was a fact that Esau had so lightly valued his birthright as to sell it to his scheming brother.... No fuller explanation of God's choice of Jacob can be found than that God delighted to love him, ... insignificant though he was."[3]

The second evidence of God's favor was that Israel had only suffered a temporary discipline in captivity while Edom had been "permanently driven out of its mountain stronghold and irretrievably banished, never to return."[4] No doubt Malachi is referring to the ransacking of the Edomites by the Nabataen Arabs, an event which would be fresh in the minds of his countrymen. By this historical intervention, God has witnessed to Israel his faithful love. He had chosen them above other people. "See how I love you," he said, "You are objects of my selective love."

Leighton Ford is fond of saying that "God loves us the way we are, but he loves us too much to leave us that way." This is a fitting context for understanding Malachi. The corrective words flow out of God's faithful commitment to love his people. It is not a word of punishment, but of correction. It is the same attitude with which Jesus Christ speaks to his church today. He loves us as his people, but he loves the church too much to leave it as it is.

Shut the Doors (Mal 1:6-14)
Malachi's first accusation was that Israel had revised God's standards of worship. They considered their worship acceptable, but God called it corrupt for four specific reasons.
Disruption in the Father-Child Relationship. First, Israel's worship was contaminated because of a disruption in the father-child relationship. The Decalog made it clear that children were to honor their parents (Ex 20:12). God, who is portrayed as both father and mother in Scripture (Is 9:6; 63:16; 64:8; 42:14; 46:3; 49:15; 66:13), parented his children from their formation in Egypt to their entrance into Canaan and finally during their exile and return to the land. But now they had begun to ignore their Father, to treat him in a way that brought disrespect to his name. There was contempt for his law and no fear of transgressing it. With the loss of respect, there was also ignorance of sin. "How have we despised thy name?" No longer sensitive to their failings, they refused to plead guilty to pollution in worship.
Offering Unacceptable Sacrifices. Israel's worship was also polluted by offering unacceptable sacrifices. Mosaic law expressly forbade the offering of blind, lame or sick animals to God (Lev 22:18-25; Deut 15:21). Sacrificial animals were to be without spot or blemish (Lev 1:3, 10; Ex 12:5). The very best was to be given to God. Yet Israel was trying to fulfill its duties with less than the best. The blind, the lame and the sick were being given to God (1:8).

Malachi taunts the people with the suggestion of giving this offering to their governor. Nehemiah in his tenure as governor did not demand food gifts or revenue from the people, but other governors did. Malachi wonders how their Persian governors would respond if they were given a sick or mutilated animal for their meal. "Will he be pleased with you or show you favor?" Such a gift would not fool the governor; it would only invite displeasure.

The brunt of God's judgment is on the Levitical priests (1:6). They as monitors and guardians of God's temple have lowered the standards to accommodate abominable offerings. Pragmatically speaking, the priests were over a barrel. Fearful of people's responses, the priests began to accept the unacceptable. If the people brought nothing, there would be no food in the priests' cupboards. Though they had no mandate to do so, they reduced the standards in order to maintain the cultus and keep their bellies full.

Wrong Thinking. Wrong thinking also polluted Israel's worship. We might say they displayed a lot of chutzpah—the kind of gall it would take for a man who had killed his parents to throw himself on the mercy of the court, pleading that he was an orphan! But this is just the sort of thing Israel was trying to do with God. They were consciously violating his commands, yet throwing themselves at his mercy because of their crop failures (2:2-3). Believing that God was obligated to bless whatever they offered, they attempted to induce his favor by prayer, fasting and the cultus. "And now entreat the favor of God, that he may be gracious to us. With such a gift from your hand, will he show favor to any of you?" (1:9). God is neither fooled, obligated nor inclined to accept uncostly worship. From the first unacceptable offering of Cain (Gen 4:5), God has made it clear that he does not grade on the curve. He has an exalted view of worship and expects us to adopt the same. God will not be manipulated or bribed into a lesser standard.

Disdainful Spirit. Finally, Israel's worship was polluted by the spirit in which it was offered. " 'What a weariness this is,' you say, and sniff at me, says the LORD of hosts" (1:13).

In our city is a large, gothic church with a series of

stained-glass windows in the south wall. Each pane has a picture of a man or woman in military dress. These windows were donated after World War 2 in honor of Canadians who died in combat. Every time I see these windows, I can't help thinking of the story of the little boy who asked his father what such windows were for. His father replied, "Those are memorials to those who died in the service." To which the boy responded, "Which service did they die in—the morning or the evening?"

Now that's not far from what Israel was experiencing. They were dying in the boredom of ritual worship. They detested going through the motions and longed to be emancipated from them. In contempt, they turned up their noses at God and said, "Here's your sacrifice. I hope you're happy with it. Now bless me so I can get out of this place and get on with life!"

The spirit of excitement, which had spurred Zerubbabel the governor and Joshua the high priest and had led to the reconstruction of the temple (Hag 1:12-15), had now dissipated. In its place hovered a languid spirit. I will never forget praying in the shower one morning, "Lord, why should going to church be such an unpleasant chore and such a frightful bore?" I did not realize what I do now: that pollution in worship quenches the presence of God's Holy Spirit, and boredom is its natural offspring.

God's unequivocal response is: "Oh, that there were one among you who would shut the doors, that you might not kindle fire upon my altar in vain! I have no pleasure in you, says the LORD of hosts, and I will not accept an offering from your hand" (1:10). God never receives unreflective, nonsacrificial worship. To maintain polluted worship only breeds a false confidence in the worshiper. But God shatters every false human confidence in order that we might come to grips with our relationship with him. The continuation of such polluted activity invites doom (1:14).

31

Both Samuel and David were clear in their understanding of what God really demands. He wants obedience before sacrifice (1 Sam 15:22). "For thou hast no delight in sacrifice; were I to give a burnt offering, thou wouldst not be pleased. The sacrifice acceptable to God is a broken spirit; a broken and contrite heart, O God, thou wilt not despise" (Ps 51:16-17). David also understood that our sacrifices must cost us something (2 Sam 24:4)—nothing easy, nothing cheap, only the very best. For the rest, God has no use. Shut the doors. Save the rituals. God has better gifts to receive.

A Word to the Priests (Mal 2:1-9)

Malachi then shifts his focus to the priests of the Levitical covenant. To appreciate the boldness with which Malachi speaks to these priests we must remember that he is one messenger speaking to other messengers. The status and importance of the priestly class in Israel should not be underestimated. As priests they were called to mediate between God and man, offering appropriate sacrifices for the sins of Israel (Lev 1—7). They were also called on to be teachers of God's law (Lev 10:11; Deut 33:10; 2 Chron 15:3). Finally, they served as judicial overseers in the resolution of legal disputes (Deut 17:9). Malachi focuses on two areas in which the priests had failed in executing their God-given mandate.

Failure to Listen. What gets your attention usually gets you. God wanted the attention of the priests in order that his Word might be taken to heart. He desired that they listen, not just for knowledge, but for obedience—not just to hear in their heads, but to hear in their hearts. God's Word is to be in our hearts before it is in sermonic outlines. There is to be no trafficking in unlived truths. When his Word has saturated our hearts, our conversation becomes the fluoroscope of our soul. We share naturally and genuinely throughout every life situation—not just from the pulpit, but at home and as we walk through the course of a daily routine.

Throughout his earthly ministry, Jesus modeled this same reflective behavior (Mk 1:35). He also urged his disciples to "come away by yourselves to a lonely place, and rest a while" (Mk 6:31). Anyone carrying on a ministry with people recognizes this need for time alone. We must come apart for a while to prevent us from coming apart permanently. We have no resources of our own to feed ourselves, let alone others. We need each day to drink deeply from the fountain of living water (Jn 7:37-39). Like squirrels we must learn to collect and store food for future days. This principle is foundational for Christian growth and ministry. Yet it is intriguing how elusive the practice is for most of us. John Wesley, in addressing a group of fellow preachers, pointed out part of the problem: "Why are we not more holy? Chiefly because we are enthusiasts, looking for the end without the means. We want lively churches, thriving evangelistic programs, and glorious worship, with social sensitivity, but we are often unwilling to pay the price for such success."[5]

One of Canada's premier evangelists of the 1940s and 50s is now a vocal agnostic. Some of his close associates mark the commencement of his downfall at the beginning of a summer holiday. Placing his Bible on the coffee table, he announced to his friends that he was tired and needed a break from God. Here his Bible would lay until he was refreshed and strengthened to read it again. But there is no real break from God nor refreshment apart from hearing his voice. The disciplines of meditation (Ps 1:2) and study (Ps 119:9-16) will demand an organized life for every leader. The cost should not be underestimated, nor the benefits. If we are not daily ingesting God's Word, we are not standing still but falling backwards. Renewed churches begin with every leader hearing from God daily.[6]

Failure to Speak. While washing my hands in a restaurant, I noticed this sign over a hot air dryer: "Push this button to hear a tape-recorded message from the Prime Minister." If we are not taking time to listen to God's voice, then our instructions will be just the same—a lot of hot air. The priests of Malachi's day were attempting to instruct without any resources. They had disregarded God's law and become laws unto themselves. Though they were given no authority to change God's Word, for convenience and necessity they substituted human wisdom and speculation as the measure of their religious life. They neglected their sacrificial duties (1:7) and also their pedagogical duties (2:7-8). In communicating God's instructions to his people they became preferential in their interpretations. Whatever was to their advantage and profit became law. By avoiding God's scrutiny of their interpretations, they fed God's people inadequate instruction. The people languished under inadequate leaders who covered up rather than revealed God's truth. As the saying goes, "When in doubt, mumble."

Failure to listen to God's Word, to honor his name and to speak his truth brings certain logical consequences. First, God promised to curse their blessing (2:2). This means either that the words pronounced by the priest over the people no longer had their power and authority (Num 6:22-27), or that the material assistance which came from the people by means of the yearly tithe would be curtailed (Num 18:21). Either way God revoked this blessing.

Second, God chose to rebuke their *offspring*. The NIV and the RSV understand this to mean "descendants." The population of Israel would suffer a decrease because of famine and warfare. Such a prediction was certainly fulfilled during the Maccabean period. Another understanding of *offspring* is "the harvest." Understood this way the rebuke of the offspring would mean no crop, no harvest, no tithe, thus starvation for the priests.

Third, so revolting to God was the offering of polluted sacrifices that he condemned the offenders to the dung hill outside the camp of Israel and thus excluded them from his presence (2:3). In humiliation and shame the priests have now become contaminated and wholly unfit for the office for which God set them apart.

Fourth, the ultimate consequence for the priests was that they would be debased in the presence of all the people (2:9). Having courted popularity by reducing God's standards, they are now despised and humiliated in the eyes of the people. Israel knew that their behavior was not according to God's pattern of holiness and would not be slow to scorn the hypocrisy of the compromising priests. God's word to Jeremiah was a word to the priests also: "But you, gird up your loins; arise, and say to them everything that I command you. Do not be dismayed by them, lest I dismay you before them" (Jer 1:17).

Priests in Midlife Crisis (Mal 2:1-16)

Not only did Israel's priests fail to listen to God's Word, but they also entered into marriages with pagans (2:11). Marriage is ordained by God and has the potential of being a spiritual catalyst. But marriage to the wrong person is one of the fastest routes to spiritual decay. When the Old Testament prohibited certain marriage arrangements, it did so not on racial but on religious grounds (Ex 34:16; Deut 7:3-4). For the testimony of God and the witness of history reveals that whenever a worshiper of Yahweh married a person from another religion the pagan standard usually prevailed. Solomon, David's son and heir to the throne, provides a classic example (1 Kings 11:1-8). The Babylonian captivity, which had occurred 125 years previous to the time of Malachi, was partially due to the apostasy brought on by interreligious marriages. Therefore, it was an abomination in God's sight for the priest to knowingly marry a "daughter of a foreign god." It was relapsing into the sin which drove them into captivity in the first place.

Malachi also attacks the priests for divorcing their older wives in order to marry younger women (2:14-16). Psychological and medical studies over the last ten years have focused attention on male midlife crisis. Popular expositions of this phenomenon usually list wife exchange as one major characteristic. Older men, longing for a new challenge to their boring existence, begin to fancy the cheap thrills of sequential polygamy. However, God's standards do not change with our age or health. Therefore, for dismissing the wives of their youth, for reneging on vows taken in his presence, God pronounces his benediction, "I hate divorce, and I hate those who attempt to cover up the gravity of their actions." The violation of the marriage vow is viewed as treachery (2:14 NASB).

The Joy of Repentance (Mal 3:7-12)
Do you use spatial language to describe your relationship with God? For example, when you are in a state of willful and persistent sin, how do you describe your relationship with God? Do you think of him as withdrawing or departing from you? If so, then you are thinking in spatial terms. Many Christians believe this to be God's way of dealing with sinful Christians. However, this understanding is deficient. God's withdrawal, if we may use the term, is not spatial, for his Spirit does not depart from believing Christians, but it is the experience we feel when we persist in sin. He is always there, patiently forgiving and directing our lives. However, our perception of his presence is obscured. Our receptors have lost their capacity for vertical fine-tuning. The interference is clearly from our side and not from God's. He cries out to us, "My love is constant. My concern never

abates. My presence does not fluctuate. But you do not comprehend it. Your persistent sin hinders you from experiencing my love and presence."

What do you do when you feel estranged from God? May I suggest a simple principle? Return to the point of your known disobedience. Receive God's forgiveness for your wayward behavior and acknowledge your present desire to live under Christ's lordship. It is when we turn to obey specifically where we have disobeyed that repentance begins and God's presence is renewed. This is Malachi's advice to Israel (3:7). They are to return to the statutes God first gave them, which they later disobeyed. When they return on God's terms, then he promises to return to them. He will bring the reality of his presence into their experience.

The return demanded of Israel is not a call to have affectionate feelings for God, to feast on his essence through the use of interior reflection, but rather to glorify him through specific acts of obedience. Christians are materialists. They believe that matter matters. Spirituality, regardless of how glorious and religious it may appear, must be rooted in the visible and material.

Israel is to return to the standards of the Sinai agreement —God's spiritual, cultic, economic and social manifesto. However, it is obvious from the context that Malachi is referring primarily to Israel's economic laws. Though we are not told specifically, violations were probably occurring in the following areas. In violation of Deuteronomy 23:19, interest was being charged to fellow Israelites. This, along with a failure to enact the seventh year remission of debt (Deut 15:1-18) and the fiftieth year of jubilee (Lev 25:8-17), resulted in an economic servitude of the worst kind. Malachi makes clear mention of the mistreatment of hired workers, again in direct violation of the law (Lev 19:13; Deut 24:14-15).

God also accuses the nation of defrauding him by withholding their tithes and offerings (3:8-9). Without the tithe, the priests, who had no allotment in the land, would soon resort to secular employment to maintain themselves and thus let the cultus sink into oblivion. The poor, as we will see later, would also suffer from the neglect of the welfare subsidy provided through a special third-year tithe. Like the farmer who hit his donkey with a fence post to get his attention, God unleashes a curse of devouring locusts to jog Israel's attention. Once he has their attention, he invites them to bring their tithe into the temple treasury. Though it appears to be a risky venture, especially when the locusts are devouring the crops, God challenges Israel to test his faithfulness to bless. With a return to tithing there is a promise of material and spiritual blessing. The blessing will be observed from distant nations who will "call you blessed." This promise again reminds us that repentance brings resounding blessing.

Preparing the Way of the Lord (Mal 4:5-6)

Some fifty years before Malachi's ministry, the prophet Zechariah announced the coming of the Lord as incentive for rebuilding the temple (Zech 8:3; 9:9). However, delay in the Lord's coming produced apathy among the people. They were tired of waiting. Returning to the same message, Malachi incorporates a new ingredient. He reveals that it is necessary for a messenger to precede the coming Lord of hosts. This messenger will arrive in the spirit and character of Elijah. According to Near Eastern customs a runner was sent in advance of an approaching king. The runner would summon the people to "prepare the way" (Is 40:3). Ruts needed to be filled in and boulders needed to be removed for the king's processional. Everything was to be made spotless for the arrival of the king.

For the Lord's coming the ruts and boulders are not

physical but relational. Before the Lord of hosts returns there must be relational restitution. Beginning within the nuclear family, there is to be a renewing of the covenant relationships between father, mother and children. Hearts made right in personal relationships then will become the pathway for God's visitation. All four of the gospel writers are convinced that John the Baptist fulfilled the predicted role of Elijah (Mt 3:3; 11:7-10; Mk 1:3-4; Lk 3:1-4; Jn 1:23). Jesus himself affirmed that John had fulfilled this ministry foretold by Malachi (Mt 11:12-15).

Purifying the Priesthood (Mal 3:2-4; 4:2-3)

In the early 1950s, Vice President Richard Nixon toured South America. One of my wife's relatives translated for Nixon during part of his journey. He remembers that as the vice president and his entourage entered each city they were greeted with freshly painted houses and fences. The slums had been given an overnight whitewash. Yet the vice president was not able to see the filth and squalor which lay behind the fences and within the houses. Malachi announces that the special visitor coming to God's people is one who is not content with external whitewashes. This kingly dignitary plans to look into every nook and cranny. Malachi wonders aloud, "Who can stand when he appears?" (3:2). When the Lord of hosts appears he will be like a laundryman who specializes in whiteness. He will know the difference between faded grays and clean whites. He will also be like a metal refiner who expects to see his own image plainly reflected in the pollutant-free molten metal. He is not coming with a superficial glance, but with an intimate analysis of all that belongs to him. Who can stand such an inspection? "Who can endure the day of his coming?"

And where will the King begin his inspection? He will come first to the priests, the sons of Levi, who have mediated between the King and his subjects. His purifying of their lives will be thorough in order that others will have a worthy model of righteousness. Then all God's people will know what is right and proper in the presence of their King.

Israel was spiritually polluted from the moment they left Egypt. Forty years of wilderness wanderings did not completely remove that pollution, nor did the correction that came during the period of the exile. But now a day is prophesied in which God will refine his people in order that they might "present right offerings to the LORD" (3:3). This day came with Jesus' death on the cross and with his dispensing of the Spirit of refinement on the day of Pentecost (Acts 2:1-4). It was the day of a new covenant, a day when stony hearts began to be replaced with sensitive hearts (Jer 31:31-34; Ezek 11:14-21). No one can go untouched by the Incarnation of Jesus Christ. His coming inaugurated refinement for some and destruction for others. There is no third category. Therefore, for the people of God refinement is seen as a sign of his elective blessing (3:17-18; 4:2-3).

Here Comes the Judge (Mal 3:5; 4:1)
For those who persist in not adjusting their lives to the dictates of the King, there will be more severe treatment. The furnace that refines will become a furnace that consumes. God does not grade on the curve. He grades with the standard of absolute righteousness and holiness. God's judgment will set aside all those who participate in cultish superstitions, who swear falsely in covenant relationships, who make themselves adulterers by sequential polygamy, who delay wages to the poor, who ignore the needs of widows and orphans, and who are unkind to sojourners passing through Israel. The arrogant and the evildoer will be consumed in the refining fire.

The Unchanging Lord (Mal 3:6, 16-18)

God shows his changeless character by his reaction to sin. The holiness of his character demands that sin should be punished. Today such activity on God's part is often viewed as cruel and unusual punishment. But let us be clear that God has created us with choice and responsibility. "Hell," said G. K. Chesterton, "is the finest compliment God could make to the dignity of human personality and to the freedom of man's choice."[7] God has announced in advance that we are accountable for our actions and will be held so at the end of time (2 Cor 5:10; Rev 20:11-15). Therefore it should not surprise us that God intends on sticking to his word.

God also does not change in his covenant relationship with his people. The covenants that God has made with his people throughout history will not be set aside. His covenant with Noah (Gen 6:18), his covenant with Abraham (Gen 12:1-3), his covenant with David (2 Sam 7:1-17) and the covenant which he inaugurated by the giving of his Son (Heb 10:15-18) will not be overturned. God in his eternal purpose has determined to prepare a people for his own glory, in order that they might "declare the wonderful deeds of him who called you out of darkness into his marvelous light" (1 Pet 2:9). To accomplish this, God faithfully commits himself to refining his people. It is fitting that the concluding words of the Old Testament should echo these two sentiments. God will not tolerate unrighteousness but will obliterate it from his presence. Moreover, he will not tolerate unrighteousness among his own people, for in his faithful character he has set about to cleanse them.

Nearly twenty-five hundred years ago, God in his great love sent Malachi to Israel. He loved his people too much to let them persist in their malodorous state. Scripture affirms that his loving concern for his people has not faltered over the years. God loves the church. He loves the church so much he has given himself for it and provided the fire-clothed Holy Spirit to produce in it the purity befitting his bride.

Although the specific sins of the church today are not those of Israel, the general categories of Malachi's prophecy do apply to us. As we prepare for the marriage feast of the Lamb (Rev 19:6-7), we will want to heed his warnings. Spotless and without wrinkle, the church is to prepare for that Day. Taking our cue from Malachi, we will in the next nine chapters examine some areas of cleansing necessary for the church to be ready for this eventful Day.

The Church's Missing Jewel

3

Before his famous circus days, P. T. Barnum ran an animal museum in lower Manhattan. People enjoyed the exhibit so much they would stay for hours, preventing other patrons from entering. Being an astute businessman, Barnam devised a method to ensure the departure of his customers who overstayed their welcome. Over the cage of the tigress and her cubs he placed a large sign, "Tigress." Then, over a doorway next to the cage, he placed another sign, "To the Egress." Thinking they would see another curiosity, many patrons trooped through the door and found themselves on the street. "Corrupt impression," says Paul Hoon, "breeds corrupt expressions."[1] It is essential, therefore, that we know what it means in biblical terms to worship God, lest we should find ourselves out on the street looking for something which does not exist.

What comes to your mind when you hear the phrase "congregational worship"? Ritualism, ceremonialism, formalism, boredom, bother, irrelevant? If any of these words strike a consonant chord, then you are probably a member of a church which has lost an important jewel; for worship, according to A. W. Tozer is "the missing jewel of the church."

Human beings were created to worship. It is as much a part of our constitution as our longing for the eternal or our sense of justice. To deny this natural response or to assume its irrelevance is like submerging a balloon under water. It continually springs up. If we are forced to suspend our worship of God, it does not mean that we stop worshiping, only that we redirect its focus toward ourselves or toward another created object rather than to the Creator.

Today, many evangelical, Bible-believing churches have denied the necessity of divine worship at the congregational level. Verbally and architecturally, the Bible has become the center of attention. The pulpit has taken over center stage. In outreforming the Reformers, the Lord's table has been pushed aside and in some cases has disappeared. The eleven o'clock worship service is really the eleven o'clock preaching hour. It is the lecture hall where sound doctrine is proclaimed, expounded and defended. But men and women, heads swimming with correct doctrine, return home unfulfilled, for they have not worshiped their Creator. One wonders if God does not likewise leave with the same questioning heart that was posed by Tevye in *Fiddler on the Roof*, "But do you love me?"

Despite these gloomy words, the evangelical church may be on the threshold of a renaissance in worship. Some churches are now in a *relational* stage where they believe that worship is telling another person what you feel about God. Others are in a *charismatic* phase of worship. They believe that worship necessitates the release of all the gifts of the Holy Spirit, moving to one collective charismatic outpouring. Still others are in a *reflective* phase of worship, where contemplation and silence are seen as the pathway to divine reverence. All these clumsy attempts are pruning the church's view of worship. Each has something to say, but none is complete in and of itself.

In looking at worship in the church today we do well to remember that fifth-century Israel likewise misunderstood, abused and neglected the worship of God. Many of the things that affected them affect the church today. Thus Malachi's words to Israel can take on significance for us: "Oh, that there were one among you who would shut the doors, that you might not kindle fire upon my altar in vain! I have no pleasure in you, says the LORD of hosts, and I will not accept an offering from your hand. For from the rising of the sun to its setting my name is great among the nations, and in every place incense is offered to my name, and a pure offering; for my name is great among the nations, says the LORD of hosts" (Mal 1:10-11).

A Call to Worship

In the history of the Christian church, Psalm 95 has traditionally been used as both a call and guide to worship. First, there is an invitation to join in exuberantly worshiping the king of salvation (vv. 1-7) which is followed by an austere reminder of the consequences of not obeying his voice (vv. 7-11).

The psalmists, when calling people to worship, occasionally suggest that we may come with either silence or tears (Ps 62:1; 65:1 NASB; 56:8). But far more often they encourage us to come before God singing and shouting joyfully (Ps 100). For many evangelicals, such activity appears too visceral for our liking. It is all right to be exuberant at a football match, but the dignity of church life demands a more subdued profile. But such thinking fails to understand the biblical flow of worship. We are to enter his gates with enthusiastic praise (Ps 95:1-5); then we are to be brought low and silent in reverential worship (Ps 95:6); and, finally, we are to arise and complete the integrity of our worship by obedience (Ps 95:7-11).

45

Praise

Israel had three main words for praise: *halal* which has to do with "making a noise" (Ps 22:23); *yadah* which was originally associated with bodily actions and gestures (Ps 111:1) and *zamar* which was playing an instrument or singing (Ps 21:13). The variety of words show us the variety of ways in which we perceive and express our appreciation to God.

God can be appreciated through the clapping of hands or the shouting out of his wonders (Ps 47:1). God can be commended by the lifting up of our eyes (Ps 123:1), by the raising of our hands (Ps 63:4; 141:2) and by dance (Ps 149:3; 150:4). He can be shown our gratitude by playing a variety of musical instruments (Ps 150), or by singing songs that have been rehearsed or songs which the Spirit has spontaneously given (Eph 5:19).

Our own church has struggled with the fulfillment of these words. We did not want to adopt a pentecostal motif, but we did want to bring more enthusiasm to our praise. We began by encouraging the use of every musical instrument in worship—not just organ and piano, but every string and woodwind instrument we could find. To this we added singers, replacing the traditional song leader or choir, who would model for the congregation an attitude of worship as well as teach new music. Our traditional hymnal was then supplemented by a host of renewal songs which have come into being within the past fifteen years, some written by our own congregation. In addition there has been drama and choreographic dance. The effect of such action has been to involve more people in contributing to worship, especially those with artistic skills. It has also freed others in the congregation to be more expressive in their praise of the Savior.

The entire Bible is punctuated with praise. Something is terribly wrong in a church that is not ringing with praise. The absence of praise is a sign of mediocre faith. In G. K.

Chesterton's words, it reveals that our religion is "more a theory than a love affair." A man must respond to the One who has given him everything. Not to do so is the highest form of ingratitude and self-sufficiency. C. S. Lewis says:

> I had never noticed that all enjoyment spontaneously overflows into praise unless (sometimes even if) shyness or the fear of boring others is deliberately brought in to check it. The world rings with praise—lovers praising their mistresses, readers their favourite poet, walkers praising the countryside, players praising their favourite game—praises of weather, wines, dishes, actors, motors, horses, colleges, countries, historical personages, children, flowers, mountains, rare stamps, rare beetles, even sometimes politicians or scholars. I had not noticed how the humblest, and at the same time most balanced and capricious, minds, praise most. . . . Except where intolerably adverse circumstances interfere, praise almost seems to be inner health made audible. . . . I had not noticed either that just as men spontaneously praise whatever they value, so they spontaneously urge us to join them in praising it: "Isn't she lovely? Wasn't it glorious? Don't you think that magnificent?" The Psalmists in telling everyone to praise God are doing what all men do when they speak of what they care about.[2]

Praise is a sign of inner health. We should not count an expression of praise to be a strange occurrence in the church. It should be a weekly corporate experience. I am amazed at the number of people who comment after leaving our church service, "I've never experienced worship like that before!"

Why are so few churches experiencing praise? Have we stopped caring about our Lord? Has peer pressure so intimidated us that we cannot speak his praises publicly? Have we so grieved the Holy Spirit that it is impossible to have enthusiasm about our Lord? If the church can take only a few scattered references as the command for world evangelism and discipleship, how can we possibly ignore the hundreds of exhortations to praise our God?

> Sing praises to God, sing praises!
> Sing praises to our King, sing praises!
> For God is the king of all the earth;
> sing praises with a psalm! (Ps 47:6-7)

Again, Lewis says: "I think we delight to praise what we enjoy because the praise not merely expresses but completes the enjoyment; it is its appointed consummation."[3] Our discipleship and our fulfillment in Christ will not be complete until our lives are alive with praise.

Worship

After exhorting us to enter God's presence with thanksgiving and praise, the psalmist urges us to "worship and bow down," to "kneel before the LORD, our Maker (Ps 95:6). As did Daniel (chap. 9) and Isaiah (6:5), we realize that we too are unworthy, sinful people in the presence of such holiness. But at the same time, as obedient people, we want to confess our omissions and transgressions. It is at this point that we need to realize that God is less concerned with pointing out our sin than he is with our grasping his wonderful character which atones for our sin (Is 6:1-7).

We move on closer to the holy of holies. As we move we are caught up in the wonder and awe of who God is. Speechless and not knowing how to respond, we can only recite the rote of the prostrate elders: "Worthy art thou, our Lord and God, to receive glory and honor and power (Rev 4:11; cf. 5:9; 7:12; 11:17). Here, repetitive and simple choruses best state the expression of our heart. This is not a time for lengthy, theological hymns. We are in his presence and want only to adore him in a language of love.

There are two principle Hebrew words used for worship in the Old Testament. One of them means to "bow down."

This bowing down is a physical sign of the reverence, awe and humility one feels in approaching God. The New Testament word *proskyneo* also carries with it this idea of prostrating oneself in awe and wonder. The other Hebrew word for worship originally signified the labor of a slave or a hired servant. This word also has a New Testament equivalent: *latreia.*

Thus worshiping God entails the humble adoration of our lips and the consecration of our lives to his service. The author of Hebrews balances perfectly this twofold call to worship: "Through him then let us continually offer up a sacrifice of praise to God, that is, the fruit of lips that acknowledge his name. Do not neglect to do good and to share what you have, for such sacrifices are pleasing to God" (Heb 13:15-16).

In modern vernacular, the word *worship* is used in a variety of ways. The mayor of our city, as well as those of other Commonwealth cities, is referred to as "his worship." We worship movie stars and musicians. We encourage self-worship through television commercials that say, "Sure it costs a little more, but I'm worth it." The term *worship* came into our speech from the Old English *weorthscipe.* This later developed into *worschipe,* then into *worship.* It means to "attribute worth" to an object or person.

Christian worship then is attributing worth to God, by the agency of the Holy Spirit, because of the work of the Son. Worship is directed to God himself not just to propositions about him. Through the blood of the Lord Jesus the veil of the temple has been pulled back (Heb 10:19-20), and with confidence in Christ as our mediator and intercessor we may enter the holy of holies and offer our verbal tribute to God.

A suggestion from Karen Mains makes this definition more concrete. Karen, who with her husband David was led into some aspects of creative worship at their church in Chicago, suggests that we begin to learn the art of verbal worship by learning to pay compliments to one another. We are unable to praise because we have lost or never possessed the verbal skills of paying compliments to anyone.

> The more our children hear compliments paid to them and then are able to give these verbal gifts to themselves, the better prepared they will be to worship God. Worship is telling God what we like about Him, telling Him what is good about His personality, or paying Him a sincere compliment. . . . My children often hear my husband and me say, "I want to tell you something I've discovered that I like about you." Or "Let me tell you what's good about you." When I draw them close for our nightly conversational prayer time, I say, "Now let's tell God some of the things that we like about Him." I am giving them a valuable tool with which to build spiritual maturity.[4]

This is certainly not all there is to worship, but for some it would be a good beginning.

Obedience
The author of Psalm 95 concludes his invitation to worship with an exhortation to obedience (vv. 6-11). We can infer from this section that one of the places in which God will speak to us about personal obedience is in the context of congregational worship. As John the apostle was in the Spirit on the Lord's day and Christ came to him with a word of correction for the Asian churches (Rev 1), so in this same context we will want to listen for personal and corporate words. These words may arise from the preaching or singing, from prayers or words of prophecy. It is then that we must take care not to harden our hearts. They must remain open and tender before the scrutiny of the Master. Then we can arise and go, knowing that our wor-

ship has integrity before God because we are prepared to obey him as Lord.

Baptized Selfism

The seventies brought on the "me generation" and the "culture of narcissism." Commercials have been quick to pick up on this preoccupation with self and have advertised with blatant call to love ourselves. In many churches this egocentricity has been baptized in the name of worship. We are now coaxed to church with phrases like "Come, you'll feel better," "Worship and you'll prosper," "Praise and you'll be healed." Christians should not be bribed to worship. A parent will often resort to bribery to get a child to finish his meal. "You'll get some nice cake if you finish your carrots." That may work for a while, but sooner or later it will fail. Without internal motivation there can be no genuine response. Likewise in worship, believers must be moved internally by the majesty of God's presence.

We must also remember the adage, "If the church marries the spirit of the age, she will be a widow in the next." We must beware lest relevancy be disclosed as secularism in religious garb. Hoon sounds this warning:

> Man's subjective preoccupation with himself, his conviction that he is the measure of things, that his individual freedom is prior to everything else, including God, and that the ultimate source of truth lies in the dramas of his own psyche rather than in any exterior revelation—this has corrupted the Church more than it realizes.[5]

As David Hubbard says, "Navel contemplation is not a fitting substitute for worship."

This accommodation to selfism is often revealed in casual and innocent words. "Did you enjoy the worship service today?" We might call this a "filling station" view of worship. The worshiper arrives at the pew ready to be refueled with all the necessary moral and spiritual encouragement to run the course for another week. But whether we enjoy it or not, are comfortable or not, are built up or not, none of these areas is a sufficient criterion for measuring worship. Rather, the test of any worship should be, "What did God receive from it? What did I put into it? Did God enjoy the worship? Was he pleased by the sacrifice of our praise and our service? Or was he discontent because our wills, emotions and intellects were disengaged in process?

There will be times when we don't care to worship God. But then we must remember that God wants costly sacrifice. Moments which cost us the most can be the greatest blessing to him. We must resist the subtle temptation to pervert the grace of God and arrange it so that for us it is cheap grace. Grace costs us nothing, but it costs God everything. We must therefore respond. We cannot sing "I Surrender All" and hold back from God our very best. We are to give all we know of ourselves to all we know of him. We must also resist the temptation to rest content with the sacrifices of others, a parasitic involvement that lets us ride the train of praise as a nonpaying stowaway.

Physically and Spiritually Fit

We cannot enter into worship unless we are physically and spiritually prepared to do so. We need to take our cue from the Jewish sabbath which begins on Friday at 6:00 P.M. We need a quiet evening of reflection and meditation in order to be contributors in corporate worship, time to restore relationships in the family, time to prepare children for their participation in worship. For the last eight years, my wife and I have zealously guarded a quiet Saturday evening, making sure that we were doing everything in our power to provide the proper soil for worship on Sunday.

Another part of our preparation for congregational worship will be the daily practice of praise and thanksgiving in our private devotions. If we are not accustomed to such a

practice, then congregational worship will be like telling a
stranger of our love in the presence of all our friends and
relatives. The unique aspect of congregational worship is
not that we do something different on a particular day, but
that on one day we do together what we have done individually throughout the week. The worship service is no place
to catch up for our lack of private praise and thanksgiving.

The Daughter of Pride

One of the greatest dangers in worship, and a signal of its
man-centered nature, is an excessive emotionalism. This is
typified in a church bulletin I saw once that announced the
following topic for the Sunday evening sermon: "Now that
you're a Holy Roller—What do you do for excitement?"
One of the greatest pollutions of our thinking about the
Holy Spirit and worship is preoccupation with feeling and
emotion. To oscillate one's diaphragm in harmony with an
eight-foot pipe or a bass guitar is not worship. Spirit-
directed worship puts no confidence in the flesh, whether
emotion or intellect. Our confidence is in the Holy Spirit
who will lead us for the edification of the body and the glory
of God. We would do well to heed John Wesley's advice
given to those who were caught up in spiritual renewal during his own ministry:

> Beware of the daughter of pride, enthusiasm. Oh, keep
> at the utmost distance from it! . . . You are in danger of
> enthusiasm every hour, if you depart ever so little from
> Scripture; yea, or from the plain literal meaning of any
> text, taken in connection with the context; and so you
> are, if you despise or lightly esteem, reason, knowledge,
> or human learnings; every one which is an excellent gift
> of God, and may serve the noblest purposes.[6]

Nevertheless, we do not need to be afraid of our emotions.
They, like the rest of our personality, can come under the
influence of the Holy Spirit. Our worship is to be joyful and

expressive. It will lead us to tears one moment and holy laughter the next. We will sing with great gusto as well as in quiet reflection. We will pray in bold praise and then be led to remain quiet. Each is controlled by the Spirit. One is not to be preferred to the other. Tom Smail says it this way:

> When the Holy Spirit moves, the destination is more important than the emotion, what we feel matters less than where we are going. We tend to be more concerned with the Spirit than He is with Himself; we can concentrate too much on His activity in us, when He is striving to point us to the origin and the end, in which the activity has its source and significance.... The Spirit moves us toward Christ.[7]

Some moments we may sense the Spirit's leading us to some participation in worship but wonder if it is not our own emotions playing tricks on us. The safest thing we can do in this situation is to ask God several times if this is his leading or just our feelings. If he is leading, then the Spirit-led intuition will remain. If it is not of him, then it will pass away in a few moments. One other check is the submission of your sensitivities to the leadership of the service or the church. We never lose by having others pray with us regarding God's leading for the body in worship.

Form and Freedom

Modern Protestants have often given interpretations to the Reformation which the Reformers never intended. For example, it is popularly held that the freedom sought in the Reformation was the "freedom to worship God as we please." But as Paul Hoon points out, nothing could be further from the truth. "The passion of the Reformers was precisely that God be worshiped as he pleased to reveal Himself in His Word."[8] It is not doing our thing, it is attempting to do God's thing. And doing God's thing means that in worship there is form and freedom. We may be opposed to formalism, but not form. We want to oppose individualistic illuminism which knows no submission to the Spirit of Christ, but we do not want to quench the freedom of the Holy Spirit. Freedom and form in worship should not be viewed as enemies, but as friends working together for the benefit of all.

The church through the centuries has held to certain forms. The Lord's Prayer (Mt 6:9-13), the vocal Amen (Neh 8:6), creedal hymns and confessions (Phil 2:6-11; 1 Tim 3:16; 2 Tim 2:11-13), the peace (Rom 16:16; 1 Cor 16:20; 1 Pet 5:14) and the Eucharist (1 Cor 11:23-26) all gave formal structure to the church in worship.

But there was also time for the exercise of the charismata (1 Cor 12—14). Paul says that when the church gathers together each one has something to give (1 Cor 14:26). It is not just the trained professionals who have prepared for the corporate gathering, but the entire church is prepared to give. They come as participants and not as spectators. Worship is not a program staged before an audience by one who has polished the fine art of communication, but rather a Spirit-inspired painting produced through a community of multigifted people who bring their own hues and colors to the service. Each can receive the fullness of the Holy Spirit, whether lay person or clergy. Each has been endowed with gifts for service. All are not exercised in one meeting, but there is room created for congregational expression. To fulfill its mandate in worship the church must resist the corruption that insists that worship is the sole responsibility of those "up front." The congregation is called not to disengaged passivity but to the Spirit-guided use of our gifts.

The practical expression of worship will vary from congregation to congregation, but the principle of multigifted participation must be maintained. For this to happen enough time must be given in the service for genuine worship. Many churches, with their overloaded schedule of Sunday school, preaching, training hour and evening service, allow little time for worship. In most churches worship is corralled into a space of about fifteen minutes including the announcements and offering. But if worship is to be an integral part of church life, we must have time to do it. We may start with only twenty minutes of the hour's service, but soon it will require an hour for fullest possible participation.

Some churches which claim to be "charismatically renewed" are really only participating in cosmetic renewal. It is just an exterior touchup. Real charismatic renewal is not just when we begin to believe in all the gifts of the Holy Spirit, but when we begin to use all the gifts of the Spirit in community under the discipline of God's Word. This type of renewal is needed in every church. If every believer-priest were emancipated to full giftedness, real church growth would soon develop. Hundreds of new churches would be springing up. Not obese churches, but stronger churches through division and multiplication. As it is now, the encouragement of passivity through the neglect of gifts leaves many churches overstaffed yet very weak. What is demanded is the full employment of every believer: "A community which allows unemployed members to exist within it will perish because of them. It will be well, therefore, if every member receives a definite task to perform for the community, that he may know in hours of doubt that he, too, is not useless or unuseable."[9]

In corporate worship the Spirit bids all the gifts to be mobilized. One will have a song, a dance, a teaching. Another will have a word of prophecy or discernment. Still others will have words of faith, knowledge and wisdom. Some will share nonverbal gifts like painting, banner making or playing a musical instrument. Yet all will be orchestrated to the praise of God the Father, through the Son, by the gifts of the Holy Spirit.

We must be careful that we are not too neat and tidy about the activity of the Holy Spirit. The immature will certainly misuse their gifts occasionally. This should not frighten us. All gifts take growth and development. They do not come to us fully developed and free of our personality. I hate to think of the poor people who endured the stumblings of my early teaching and preaching ministry. The same acceptance that was extended to me now needs to be given to those who have a gift of spontaneous song, dance, words of prophecy, visions or dreams. We should be encouraging, supportive and corrective in receiving these various gifts in worship. They are all to abound to his glory.

In 1977, the Evangelical Council of the Anglican Church (England) and the Fountain Trust produced a working paper on "The Gospel and the Spirit." There were a number of leading evangelical Anglicans who signed the document, including John Stott and J. I. Packer, as well as those who represented a more charismatic view of the Church. Their statement on worship attempts to hold together both freedom and form:

> We believe that what are seen as characteristic features of "evangelical" and "charismatic" worship and spirituality will complement and enrich one another and correct the imbalances in each, although we recognise that in some situations the two so overlap already as to be almost indistinguishable. Many "charismatic" gatherings would benefit from order, teaching, and some robustly doctrinal "evangelical" hymns; just as many "evangelical" services and prayer meetings would benefit from more spontaneity, greater participation, a more relaxed atmosphere, the gentle, loving wonder and praise of some renewal songs, and learning to listen to God in times of prayer and meditation.[10]

Is there leadership in such services? Most certainly there is. But it is a leadership that works both within the form and allows for freedom. The leader is analogous to the conductor of a symphony orchestra. In no way does he attempt to call attention to himself or to prohibit any of the instruments from playing their scores, but rather he serves the orchestra by guiding it into an harmonious symphonic sound. His job is not to produce the sound. God by his Spirit will create worship in people's hearts. The leader must simply be sensitive to the Spirit who is harmonizing that worship.

The church must hold in tension the necessity of having both form and freedom. We must risk the benefit of both. To those who have no formal structure for worship, the New Testament calls us back to a weekly Eucharist. To those whose liturgies allow no freedom, the New Testament calls us to the use of the charismata. Many of our structures are not so biblical as they are traditional and cultural. To make them into absolutes that have no flexibility is idolatry.

In Truth and Spirit

Jesus, in his dialog with the Samaritan woman at the well of Sychar, spoke of an impending hour in which "true worshipers will worship the Father in spirit and truth" (Jn 4:23). This is how God chooses to be worshiped, not according to manmade plans and human wisdom, but in response to his Spirit in accordance with Scripture. We are not given carte blanche on any religious experience. What we experience must have the marks of Jesus to be a valid expression of the Spirit. There should be spontaneity, liberty and joy. There should also be submission to God's revelation to correct our propensity for placing confidence in ourselves. We must remember that we "worship in the Spirit of God and glory in Christ Jesus and put no confidence in the flesh" (Phil 3:3 NASB). We cannot assume that our worship is pleasing to God unless we let the Holy Spirit have his full control of our lives. Without his activity there can be no worship of Jesus Christ, for the Spirit is the traffic director in the flow of worship. God gives himself to us in Christ through the Spirit, and we give ourselves in the Spirit through Christ to God the Father.

We need both Word and Spirit—not one to the exclusion of the other: "All Word and no Spirit—we dry up; all Spirit and no Word—we blow up; Word and Spirit—we grow up."[11]

D. L. Moody once commented that he would not "put live chicks under a dead hen." Interpreted by evangelicals this has meant the necessity of sending young converts to a church which preached the Bible as the Word of God. A church uncommitted to the teaching of the Scriptures, like a dead hen, would soon smother the growth of any new Christian. I have sympathy for such a principle. However, I should like to add: Don't send young converts to a church which corrupts worship either by neglect or abuse. What the church is doing in heaven is what the church ought to be doing on earth (Rev 4:1-11; 5:1-14). Our destiny is the worship of our Savior. Every mention of elders in the book of Revelation shows them at worship. It is to this end that we should prepare ourselves now—not just sound in doctrine, but also flowing with praise, for the two together provide fertile soil for growth of any new believer.

Remember Me, Sometime

4

I was at one of those luncheons evangelicals give for other evangelicals to promote their hardware. Big names were everywhere. Across from me sat several journalists from Christian magazines. One of these reporters was a young critic, notorious for exposing the faults of evangelicalism. Next to him sat an elderly man who was later described in the meeting as the "dean of American New Testament Scholarship." Not intending to eavesdrop, I nevertheless overheard a rather revealing comment. Early in the meeting the critic turned to the "dean" and said, "What is your name?" The elderly man graciously answered, and the young man went on, "And what do you do?" I could not but chuckle how this critic had lost all contact with his historical roots as an evangelical. The "dean," who had contributed so much, was unknown to this contemporary commentator.

In May 1977 forty-five evangelicals from a variety of backgrounds gathered near Chicago to issue the now famous "Chicago Call," calling evangelicals back to their historic roots.

We confess that we have often lost the fullness of our

Christian heritage, too readily assuming that the Scriptures and the Spirit make us independent of the past. In so doing, we have become theologically shallow, spiritually weak, blind to the work of God in others and married to our cultures.[1]

Strange as it appears, evangelicals who formerly took no thought for the traditions of the church are now finding that such traditions are absolutely essential for the renewal of the church. For example, section five of "The Chicago Call" was entitled "A Call to Sacramental Integrity."

We decry the poverty of sacramental understanding among evangelicals. This is largely due to the loss of our continuity with the teaching of many of the Fathers and Reformers and results in the deterioration of the sacramental life in our churches. Also, the failure to appreciate the sacramental nature of God's activity in the world often leads us to disregard the sacredness of daily living.

Therefore we call evangelicals to awaken to the sacramental implications of creation and incarnation. For in these doctrines the historic church has affirmed that God's activity is manifested in a material way. We need to recognize that the grace of God is mediated through faith by the operation of the Holy Spirit in a notable way in the sacraments of baptism and the Lord's Supper. Here the church proclaims, celebrates and participates in the death and resurrection of Christ in such a way as to nourish her members throughout their lives in anticipation of the consummation of the kingdom. Also, we should remember our biblical designation as "living epistles," for here the sacramental character of the Christian's daily life is expressed.[2]

Doubtlessly, many of us greet such a statement with mixed emotions—the feeling you get when your mother-in-law drives over a cliff driving your new Cadillac. There are some things we like and some we would prefer not to discuss. However, this call beckons us to examine whether or not we are properly handling the sacred institutions that were established by our Lord. In Malachi's words, are we teaching "that the LORD's table may be despised" (Mal 1:7)?

The Lord's Supper

The sacrament of the Lord's Supper is known by various names in different traditions. Most of these terms find their source within the New Testament. From 1 Corinthians alone there are four possible descriptions. It can be referred to as the "Lord's Supper" (11:20), a "remembrance service" (11:24), the "Eucharist" (which comes from the Greek word for giving thanks in 11:24) or "Communion" (10:16). All four terms are appropriate to describe this visible symbol of the New Covenant.

Jesus instituted this meal during the Passover feast during the last week of his earthly life. Generally the church has concluded that the Jewish Passover (Ex 12) provides the indispensable key to an understanding of the Lord's Supper. God, in his severity and mercy, afflicted Egypt with death but passed over Israel because of the blood of the sacrificial lamb which was placed on the doorpost and lintels of Jewish homes. The sacrificial lamb was eaten in its entirety. Israel packed its stores of unleaven bread in preparation for a hasty departure from their captivity. Year after year, Israel paused at the Passover meal to remember God's provision for their release. Jesus, the heaven-sent Lamb of God, was now preparing to have his body broken and his blood shed "on the behalf of many for the forgiveness of sins." In the Upper Room, Jesus continues the tradition of the Passover meal, only giving it its ultimate significance by his own death.

With the establishment of the church at Pentecost, we learn that the early Christians broke bread in their homes

(Acts 2:42, 46; 20:7). This meal was initially known as the agape or "love feast" (Jude 12). Though there is no mention of wine in the Acts references, there is little doubt that the Christians reflected on their crucified and risen Lord at these table meals. Later in the church's history, the agape meal was separated from a more formal participation in the Lord's Supper. Sunday, "the Lord's Day" (Rev 1:10), was not observed as a public holiday until the fourth century under Constantine. Before this time, Christians met early in the morning for worship. This service included praise and thanksgiving, Bible reading, prayer and preaching before partaking in the bread and wine. The agape meal was preserved as an evening fellowship until the third and fourth century.

Paul, by revelations from Jesus Christ, lays out an orderly progression for participation in the Lord's Supper (1 Cor 11:23-26).

Eucharist. First is the Eucharist, or the giving of thanks (v. 24). The church, after participating in a period of spontaneous praise and thanksgiving (1 Cor 14:26), is led in a corporate thanksgiving for the cup and the loaf. The Didache, also called The Teaching of the Twelve Apostles, a second-century manual for Christian behavior, prescribes the following prayers of thanksgiving:

> Now concerning the giving of thanks. Give thanks in the following manner. First, concerning the cup: "We thank you, our Father, for the holy vine of David your servant, which you have made known to us through Jesus your Servant. Glory to you forever!" And concerning the broken loaf: "We thank you, our Father, for the life and knowledge which You have made known to us through Jesus your Servant. Glory to you forever! (9:1-3)

There was also to be thanksgiving at the end of the meal.

> We thank you, Holy Father, for your holy Name which you have made to dwell in our hearts; and for the knowl-

edge and faith and immortality which you have made known to us through Jesus your Servant. Glory to you forever! You, Almighty Master, created everything for your Name's sake; you have given food to men for their pleasure so that they might give you thanks. And to us you have graciously given spiritual food and drink and life eternal through Jesus your Servant. Most of all, we thank you, because you are mighty. Glory to you forever! (10:1-4)[3]

Remembrance. Paul teaches that the Lord's Supper was to be done in remembrance of Jesus Christ (vv. 24-25). As the church celebrated this meal each week they recalled the atonement for sin made at Calvary's tree. However, this remembrance was not just a mental activity of recollection, but as F. F. Bruce states, it was "a realization of what is remembered. At the Passover feast the participants are one with their ancestors of the Exodus; at the Eucharist, Christians experience the real presence of the Lord."[4] Jesus, formerly crucified is now the risen, living Lord.

"In remembrance of me," then, is no bare historical reflection of the Cross, but a recalling of the crucified and living Christ in such a way that He is personally present in all the fulness and reality of His saving power, and is appropriated by the believer's faith.[5]

Proclamation. The Lord's Supper is also proclamation (v. 26). Corporate participation in the Lord's Supper became an act of preaching. Augustine spoke of this sacrament as an "acted-out sermon." It was proclamation through the use of symbols rather than the spoken word. The word translated "proclaim" is used in other places to describe the verbal announcement of the gospel (1 Cor 2:1; 9:14). Though typically it is not, the Eucharist should be seen as a vital launching pad for the church in its mission to the world. The proclamation at the Eucharist is also a proclamation of hope. Through it participants affirm the

second advent of Jesus Christ, "until He comes."
Communion. Last, the Lord's Supper is communion: "Is not
the cup of blessing which we bless a sharing [communion]
in the blood of Christ? Is not the bread which we break a
sharing [communion] in the body of Christ? Since there is
one bread, we who are many are one body; for we all partake of the one bread" (1 Cor 10:16-17 NASB). The Eucharist is communion with our Lord, by his Spirit through
faith, and communion with fellow believers in the body of
Christ. Robert Webber notes at least one reason for our
failure to grasp the significance of these words:

> The emergence of post-renaissance individualism has re-
> placed the corporate experience of the church around
> the body and blood of Christ with the individual experi-
> ence of salvation. This introduction of individualism with
> the simultaneous loss of the communal aspect of the
> Eucharist has had ramifications particularly in our loss of
> the Church as the body of Christ. Interestingly, the cur-
> rent recovery of the body of Christ is attended by the re-
> covery of worship, particularly the Eucharist where the
> single body of Christ gathers in union around signs of
> redemption.[6]

We partake of one loaf because we are one body under one
Lord. The severe restrictions on intercommunion among
Christians in both high and low church traditions are a rebuke to Christ's lordship over one body and a visible sign to
the world of the church's corruption. Jesus, before he died,
prayed for the unity of the church (John 17:20-26) and now
in heaven intercedes for the same end. Do we not need to
repent of our petty divisions and pray the Eucharistic
prayer of the Didache? "Just as this loaf previously was scattered on the mountains and when it was gathered together
it became a unity, so may your Church be gathered together
from the ends of the earth into your kingdom. For glory
and power are yours forever, through Jesus Christ" (9:4).

Absence Makes the Heart Grow Cold

In some evangelical churches today, it is possible for a believer to go months and even years without participation in the Lord's Supper. We cannot fool ourselves by believing that the call to Eucharistic celebration is given only to those who are sacramentally inclined. We are commanded to partake of this supper with him. "Do this in remembrance of me" (1 Cor 11:24-25). It is one of the clearest injunctions given to the church to maintain until Christ returns. To disregard it is sheer disobedience. To fail to observe it will only enhance our dearth of thanksgiving, remembrance, proclamation and communion.

For those committed to observance of the Lord's Supper, the question of frequency remains. As I have said, initially the Lord's Supper was taken informally around a meal with believing friends and relatives. This was often done on a daily basis. At the same time, the church in its corporate gathering remembered the Lord every Sunday. As Luke writes, "And on the first day of the week, when we were gathered together to break bread..." (Acts 20:7). A century after this reference to the believers at Troas, the church was still maintaining the practice of weekly Communion, for we read in the Didache, "And when you gather together each Lord's day, break bread and give thanks" (14:1). If this was the practice of the first two centuries of the church, why have segments of the evangelical church today lost the significance of this activity? History reveals that the answer is twofold: first, the exaggerated holiness of the Communion clements frightened people from participation, and second, the practical outworking of the Reformation was to replace the sacrament of the Eucharist with the sacrament of the Word.

You might be wondering what could have frightened the church from participation in the Lord's Supper. It is difficult to trace the origins of this problem, but we can see by the medieval period that church leaders had altered the affirmation of Christ's real presence at the Eucharist and substituted for it a view that the bread and wine became the substance of Christ's body and blood. This was later known as transubstantiation. Some eleventh-century theologians actually maintained that if "you bite the bread you have bitten the body of Christ." To them, Jesus' words in John 6:52-59 were literally fulfilled in the Eucharist. Therefore, Christians needed to be extremely cautious about handling the body and blood of our Lord. Hence, a protectorate priest class became necessary to handle the feeding and monitor the frequency.

One other element was present in this prereformation theology: the belief that a person needed to be worthy before partaking in the sacrament. Thus fear and a sense of unworthiness combined to lessen the frequency with which the laity actually took part at the Lord's table. It was no longer a daily or weekly event, but more likely only a yearly celebration. It was not important to participate in the Mass, only to be present at it. The yearly intake of spiritual vitamins was all that was necessary for immortality. As you can see, the church was eventually theologically and emotionally disenfranchised from the Lord's Supper. As part of the Reformation drive in Geneva in 1536, John Calvin attempted to reinstitute the Lord's Supper as part of the church's weekly life. This was met with opposition from church officials. However, a compromise of quarterly Communion was arranged. This practice is still common in some churches today; however, most evangelical churches practice Communion on a monthly basis. This again is not because of any particular scriptural merit, but simply as a compromise to the prereformation taboo of frequent Communion.

The argument that familiarity breeds contempt is often brought against those who practice weekly Communion. I once heard a preacher harangue for an hour on the potential abuses of frequent Communion. But God, as G. K. Chesterton reminds us, is strong enough to exult in monotony. Regarding Israel's cultic practices he never said: "You people ought not sacrifice to me daily, it is boring me. Besides it's going to get very old soon and you will begin to pollute the whole institution." Rather, he always reminded them through the prophets that their hearts must be right for their sacrifices to be effective. Likewise, Jesus did not tell the church to abstain from a weekly Eucharist lest we corrupt it, but rather in love and harmony with our neighbors, we are to remember him (Mt 5:23-24; 1 Cor 11:28).

Another reason for the church's failure to celebrate weekly Communion is the belief that the Reformation replaced the sacrament of the Eucharist with the sacrament of the Word. But the Reformers were not out to dismiss the Eucharist from the liturgy of the church, only to bring it back into conformity with the Scriptures:

> To imagine that Calvin wished to replace sacramental worship by a preaching service is to completely misunderstand his mind and work and to ignore all that he taught and did. His aim was twofold: to restore the Eucharist in its primitive simplicity and true proportions —celebration and communion—as the central weekly service; and within this service, to give the Holy Scriptures their authoritative place. The Lord's Supper, in all its completeness, was the norm he wished to establish.[7]

The evangelical church has not listened to this Reformed emphasis and has comforted itself with the exclusive use of the audible sacrament—sitting and listening to the Word of God. Praise God that his Word is being taught! But an overemphasis on preaching and the neglect of worship in the Lord's Supper is like an overweighted kite tail: though given for stability, it ends up as an accomplice in the destruction. God's people need, want and are commanded to worship. Preaching is to give guidance to that worship so that it is worship "in truth." But the exclusive use of a one-dimensional preaching sacrament, God to his people through his Word and servant, is a denial of true worship. It is what Karl Barth called a "torso" service, a worship service which has been mutilated because of the lack of the Eucharist. Both sacraments are intended to feed God's people. Christ is to be perceived everywhere, in our ears, eyes, minds, hearts, hands and mouths.

C. S. Lewis once commented that "a man cannot always be defending the truth; there must be a time to feed on it." The celebration of the Lord's Supper gives God's people an opportunity to feed on the truth of God's redeeming them through Christ. We feed on God's love and acceptance as it was demonstrated on the cross. As Bob Tuttle has said, "We can't mess up bad enough to make God love us less, and we can't work hard enough to make Him love us more."

The ultimate basis for any positive self-image will be God's acceptance of us in Christ. If he has accepted us, we are obliged to accept ourselves. God says that he has forgiven us all sins—past, present and future. He is the only propitiation for sin, and we are the recipients of his work (1 Jn 2:1). He has paid the price of our redemption. We are freed from our true moral guilt and bondage to sin (Rom 6:6), and are destined now to live only for the praise of his glory (Eph 1:6). Nothing can separate us from his love (Rom 8:35). The world is already in his triumphant hand. The battle has been fought. Satan is defeated. Christ is Victor. With such thoughts, both personal and cosmic, we feed on the Supper placed before us.

Their Eyes Were Opened

I have a friend who loves to go on long meditative walks. At a conference in Alberta, he decided to go for one of his walks with a companion. Several miles away the companion began to tire, so they decided to hitchhike home. A young bearded man picked them up and was driving them home. After several miles, my friend, who had been in animated conversation with his walking companion, asked the young driver his name. The young man said, "Dad, I'm your son Alf." The new-grown beard and disinterest in the driver had kept him from seeing his own son.

Similarly, the two disciples on the Emmaus road failed to recognize the risen Savior (Luke 24:13-35). Even after he gave them an extended treatment of the suffering and glory of the Messiah, they still did not perceive who was speaking to them. But when Jesus sat down at the table and broke bread with them, "their eyes were opened and they recognized him." Since this first postresurrection meal, the church has always contended that Jesus is present at the breaking of the bread. He is met in the sacrament. He is not dead and gone, but alive and present. At every meal in which he is remembered, he is there by his Spirit. Not in the crass manner of transubstantiation, but in a real presence which the church refused to explain other than as an operation of faith.

Under Zwingli, Protestant scholasticism reduced the undefinable real presence into a mere memorial or symbol —a symbol of the past with no special dynamics for the present. But one wonders if this rationalism has not lost for us the presence of God at the table. Tom Howard holds that this is true and argues for a return to the "one whole fabric" view of the sacraments:

Sacramentalism may be understood then, as the view that sees a discernible meeting point in appointed physical vehicles between visible and invisible realms. Put another way: Sacramentalism rejects sheer dualism, if by this we understand that the universe is forever divided utterly between the temporal and the eternal, or the material and the spiritual, or the visible and the invisible realms. It rejects much of popular Platonism, that "reality" is located wholly in the spiritual realm, and that the material world is illusion.... For at the foundation of sacramental vision lies the robust affirmation of the whole creation, from seraphim to clams to basalt, as *one good fabric.*[8]

By means of his Spirit, Christ is with us in the Eucharist. The invisible and visible are as one. We eat the bread and drink the wine and thus feed on him.

Going with the Flow

Robert Webber, in tracing the theological structure of worship in the third and fourth centuries, suggests a basic pattern.[9] I was amazed when I first saw this chart. Our community had been following this pattern for three years in our morning service and at that time was considering changing it in order to accommodate more people in our small building. The proposed change failed to gain approval from the congregation who felt the balance and flow of the service were perfect. The structure of the morning looks something like this:

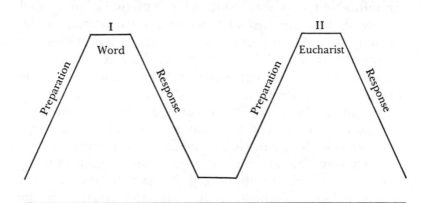

Phase I begins with singing and prayer, preparing our hearts to hear God's Word. We often sing this simple chorus before the teaching of the Word: "Bless thy Word unto our hearts and glorify thy name. Glorify thy name, Lord. Bless thy Word unto our hearts and glorify thy name." This is followed by thirty-five to forty minutes of expository preaching. At the end of the sermon, the desired response to God's Word is often spelled out—an invitation to come to Christ, a call for reconciliation, congregationally led prayers of commitment, or hymns or choruses given as verbal contracts of personal commitment.

Phase II begins with praise and thanksgiving. As we move to the table, into the heart of worship, we are led in a quieter and more reflective manner. Simple songs that express devotion and adoration lead us to the table: "How I love thee, precious Savior," "Jesus, Lamb of God, have mercy upon me" or "Jesus, name above all names." Prayers of thanksgiving are offered for the elements, and we meet Jesus in the bread and wine. Our response may be of testimony or song or a time to pray for the needy in our community. Our financial offering is the next response, followed by the benediction. The entire process takes nearly two hours. Surprisingly, people are not exhausted from such an exercise, but seemingly delightfully refreshed as they have been fed by God's Word and God's Supper.

The church has always celebrated the Lord's Supper as the focal point of worship. Neither preaching, charismatic praise, nor silent contemplation is a fitting substitute for this practice. We need each of these in our worship service. But we also need weekly participation in the Lord's Supper. Jesus chooses to meet us at this station of grace. We do him great dishonor to ignore it or disobey it. This Supper is not offered to us on the basis of our own merit. We come only in the worth of Christ, spotless and without blame because of his sacrificial and substitutionary death. It is only incum-

73

bent on the communicants that they be reconciled with their brothers and sisters before they take the elements. And though the paradox of his presence at the table while at the same time at the right hand of the Father strains our imagination, we are commanded to meet him there, and by faith we are able to do so. "He was recognized by them in the breaking of the bread" (Lk 24:35 NASB).

Fair Beauty of the Lord
In chapters two and three I tried to show failures present in evangelical worship. Each of these areas hinders God's name from being great among the nations (Mal 1:11). There is a direct link between our worship and our evangelistic impact. As C. S. Lewis has said, "I did not see that it is in the process of being worshipped that God communicates His presence to men. It is not of course the only way. But for many people at many times the "fair beauty of the Lord" is revealed chiefly or only while they worship Him together."[10]

In unpolluted worship, the "fair beauty of the Lord" is revealed to all those who are present. As with Moses on Mount Sinai, the congregation, in Spirit-directed worship is engulfed in theophany. God's presence descends in the midst of his people. The God who is there has become the God who is here. He is here in all his immanent glory. We are no longer talking about him; we are talking to him. And by means of his Word, his eucharistic grace and the gifts of his Holy Spirit, God communicates with us. In that environment, non-Christians who previously have been Word-resistant are brought forcefully face to face with God the Creator and Redeemer. They must choose whom they will serve, not because they are psychologically exhausted through tireless altar calls, but because God is there and he is calling them to repentance. Hoon expresses my concern well when he says:

The congregation rather than the individual Christian

is to be seen as the true agent of evangelism, and its worship—especially Holy Communion—as the place par excellence where evangelical action is beheld in its true essence. Here the Lord's saving death is proclaimed with unique power, and the life of the New Age released into the old order of decay, sin, and death. And here likewise is the pivotal reality, The Event of Jesus Christ, that saves evangelism from becoming ecclesiastical propagandizing. In short, liturgy as the showing forth of the Gospel is the heart and motive of authentic evangelism. . . . Authentic worship, if we only realized it, is one of the most powerful forms of mission and evangelism the Church can employ.[11]

Several passages of Scripture reveal the impact of our worship on non-Christians. The first is from the mouth of David as he recalls God's rescuing him from "the pit of destruction": "He put a new song in my mouth, a song of praise to our God. Many will see and fear, and put their trust in the LORD" (Ps 40:3). Is that not what God has done for us in Jesus Christ? Has he not rescued us from a "pit of destruction"? Has he not put "a new song in our mouth"? Then should we not expect that some would see this work of God in the restoration of our lives and turn to him? Indeed we should expect it to be so.

The second passage comes from the day of Pentecost. Having been filled with the fullness of God's presence through the indwelling of the Holy Spirit, the disciples are compelled to declare "the mighty works of God" (Acts 2:11). Praise has an evangelistic function, though that is not its primary function. And praise, combined with the preaching of the gospel, and not one without the other, sees a harvest of three thousand new converts. The church in worship is the fountain which flows with evangelistic power and the summit to which her activity leads.[12] Preaching the gospel is important; but, as Michael Green has said, "Let our preaching be an explanation of the worship which is demonstrated." Let us preach and answer questions that have been raised by our joy and infectious praise.

In the last few years I have been in a number of churches thinking about evangelism and worship. Some of these churches decided to declare a moratorium on extensive evangelism, simply because they could not accommodate any more new Christians. They were suffering from manna panic. They were not products of church-growth techniques nor coparticipants in any large evangelistic thrust. They were simply going about doing their job of being the church, and God "was adding to their numbers daily." People were drawn to Christ by joyful, worshiping, loving Christians. Intelligent, joyful worship is an infallible sign of the presence of God.

Returning Glory

Calvary Chapel in Costa Mesa, California, came into national prominence during the Jesus movement of the late 1960s. Today the church ministers to about 15,000 people each Sunday. I have visited the church on many occasions and have found it to have a healthy balance in its attempts at renewal in worship. To summarize what I want to emphasize about worship I am reproducing here a brief description found in their Sunday bulletin several years ago with one addition, that on the sacrament of the Lord's Supper:

We believe worship of God should be spiritual.

Therefore: We remain flexible and yielded to the leading of the Holy Spirit to direct our worship.

We believe worship of God should be inspirational.

Therefore: We give a great place to music in our worship.

We believe worship of God should be intelligent.

Therefore: Our services are designed with great emphasis upon teaching the Word of God that he might instruct us how he should be worshiped.

We believe worship of God should be sacramental.

Therefore: We give ourselves to weekly observance of the Lord's Supper.

We believe worship of God is fruitful.

Therefore: We look for his love in our lives as the supreme manifestation that we have truly been worshiping him.

May God bring renewal to our worship, that many might "see and fear and turn to the Lord."

Who's in Charge Here?
5

Walt Disney immortalized the story of a faithful pup by the name of Greyfriars' Bobby. The exceptional devotion of this canine led him to continue guarding his master's grave for some fourteen years after his death. While we were touring in Edinburgh one afternoon, some friends who knew the story wanted to visit the memorial to this faithful pooch. Though I was not particularly excited about the venture, I was persuaded to follow the group in their search for the statue. For some strange reason I had it in my mind that the memorial would be the size of the lions in Trafalgar Square. When we arrived at the cemetery, the search began. I drifted off, reading headstones in the cemetery until suddenly I realized that I had lost my companions. Rendezvousing with them, I saw that they had stumbled on the memorial we were looking for. But much to my surprise, Greyfriars' Bobby was not at all the size of the Trafalgar Square lions. Sitting on its concrete base, the statue was barely eighteen inches high.

After taking a few snapshots and walking back to the hotel, I began to think how my distorted image was a fitting example of our search for leadership in the church. I began to ask myself, Who could match up to the Apostles? Who could really fulfill the description of an elder in 1 Timothy 3? Who could follow in the steps of Calvin, Spurgeon, Moody and others? I also asked, Does the church need the Trafalgar lions, the "superstar pastors"? Or do we need more "puppies of Edinburgh"?

My frank conviction is that the church today needs not more evangelical giants or media superstars, but thousands more simple, dedicated folk who may have no natural charisma but who do have the spiritual commitment and strength to lead the kingdom fight against the evil one, men and women who have taken seriously the calling of leading God's people. If the church is to be renewed, it will need renewed leadership. Corrupt leadership will only result in a corrupt populace and an ineffective church. As Malachi sounded his warning to the leadership of fifth-century Israel, so today similar warnings need to be given to the church.

The New Covenant inaugurated by Jesus' death on the cross brought with it a new plan for the leadership of God's people. No longer was leadership confined to one priestly class distinct from the rest of the people of God. The new order proclaims all believers to be priests (1 Pet 2:5, 9; Rev 1:6). Male and female, adult and child, all serve as ministers before God. This change, however, does not mean that the church is leaderless or totally egalitarian. Yet the question of what form and structure this leadership should take divides Christendom. With the deluge of titles and offices that have filled the church, it is time we take another look at what the New Testament teaches on the leadership of Christ's body. First, in this chapter we will see from the words of Jesus that leadership is rooted in the concept of servanthood (Mt 20). Second, in chapter six we will see from Paul's words to Timothy that leadership of a local church rests in the character and gifts of elders.

Searching for the Head
One Sunday morning a mother handed me a slip of paper recording this humorous little incident. During dinner the previous night the following conversation took place among three of her children.

Geoffrey: Do the Mallones go to our church?

Betsy: That's Eryn Faye and Scott's mom and dad!

Jenny: Of course they do. Mr. Mallone is the head of our church.

Geoffrey: And Mr. Dorman, too?

Jenny: Well, sort of. He sets up the chairs. Mr. Mallone is there every day so he's the head of our church.

This childlike expression reveals the constant pressure the church is under to have a head.

Recently I read a survey regarding the type of leadership people want in the church today. The conclusion of the survey was that people were tired of the Dagwood Bumstead model, the Caspar Milquetoast who is pushed from pillar to post. They would prefer the relaxed, loving and disciplined style of John Walton. But if worse came to worst, they would settle for Archie Bunker. In the same week one pastor confessed to me that, because of the need for authority, men were now becoming pastors in his denomination who formerly went into the Royal Canadian Mounted Police.

The Cornerstone of New Testament Leadership
In Matthew 20:20-28, Jesus utters some of the most radical words ever heard regarding leadership. Throughout much of church history these words have been only dimly perceived. Yet these words form the cornerstone of New Testament leadership. Jesus promised his disciples that when he was ruling on his throne they would also be upon their

thrones judging the twelve tribes of Israel (Mt 19:29). It appears, however, that such a reward was not sufficient for James and John. The struggle for rank and privilege which had been characteristic of the disciples in their early days had now come to a head. Having an inside track, the sons of Zebedee sent their mother Salome to speak to Jesus. If John identifies the same people as Mark at the cross, then Salome (Mk 15:40) is Jesus' mother's sister (Jn 19:25). It might appear then that cousins James and John suggested that Aunt Salome might have a better chance of seeing their request adopted. After all, blood is thicker than water. She approached Jesus and requested that her sons be given the positions of privilege in the throne arrangement, that they might sit next to the seat of power and authority. Rather than rebuking James and John, Jesus posed them a question. Were they able to undergo the experience of suffering and abuse that was his own destiny? As a measure of their loyalty, they announced that they were prepared for such sufferings. In predicting their destiny, Jesus replied that they would drink the cup. James soon became the first Christian martyr, and John was later banished to the island of Patmos. But to designate heavenly honor is the prerogative of the Father, and Jesus refused to overrule his design. The remaining ten were indignant at this power play by James and John. In this revelation of selfish, raw ambition Jesus began to teach on leadership in the church.

Leading by Lording
"But Jesus called them to him and said, 'You know that the rulers of the Gentiles lord it over them, and their great men exercise authority over them' " (Mt 20:25). This verse provides for us a summary of secular authority. Regardless of whether it is exercised in the church or in the political arena, it is essentially oppressive, self-directed power. People who have spent all their energies getting to the top now

let others feel the full weight of their authority. They lord it *over* others and are concerned to exercise authority *over* others. They are preoccupied with position. Luke says that these people are called "benefactors" (Lk 22:25). They "love" their people by keeping an oppressive heel on the back of their necks. Words of affection flowed from men like Idi Amin, the Shah of Iran and Jim Jones, when all along they really were oppressive potentates.

These are harsh political and cult examples, but there are milder and more subtle forms within the church. There are those who pressure us to believe that the church is a business corporation with a director at the top. Everyone is to jump when the boss speaks. To others it is the professor who knows Greek and Hebrew and who alone can untangle for us the mysteries of Scripture. To others it is the man or woman who has pastoral gifts of discernment and prophecy, who demand that their disciples be obedient to the vision which they have for them.

In the last few years, both charismatic and evangelical churches have been split over the "shepherding controversy." In its extreme, it is extortion and domination of the worst variety. Seen in its best light it is a response to the crass individualism of many North American Christians. The question that is being asked is, How are we to shepherd people unless they are responsive to our authority? No doubt, the majority of those asking this question are genuinely concerned for the believers under their charge (Heb 13:17; 1 Pet 5:1-5). However, the movement has created alarm by its failure to understand the potential sinfulness of leadership within the church. It is only one small step from "pastoral leadership to spiritual domination" and from "biblical submission to communitarian subservience."[1] What is true of Lord Acton's phrase in politics is also true in religion. "All power tends to corrupt, and absolute power corrupts absolutely."

Often leaders begin to believe things of themselves that are essentially lies. They develop an inflated and infallible view of themselves. Malcolm Muggeridge, going into one of the storage rooms in a London wax museum, found no less than six heads of Prime Minister Harold Wilson. When he asked why there were six heads, he was told that during his period of office Wilson's head grew steadily bigger. It was thus necessary to redo it from time to time. "Why keep all six used heads?" Muggeridge then asked. Because once out of office Wilson's head would likely shrink and the old heads would come in handy.

Anyone with the least pastoral experience will confirm that when people take their eyes off of Jesus Christ and begin to focus them on some human leader, the leader's own importance is apt to be inflated and the faith of the people rests on woefully shaky ground. After watching the newsreel of the death of Pope John Paul I, my three-year-old son went and hid himself in the bedroom. A few minutes later I discovered him crying. When I asked him what the problem was, he answered that he was sad because "the hope was dead." Whenever we look to leadership in a single person, a discipler or teacher or whatever, our hopes can easily be dashed with the failings of that person. Our eyes are to be on Jesus. He is the one and only head of the church. He does not share his lordship over the church with anyone. He is the exclusive head and mediator to every man, woman and child within the church.

Leading by Serving

"It shall not be so among you; but whoever would be great among you must be your servant, and whoever would be first among you must be your slave; even as the Son of man came not to be served but to serve, and to give his life a ransom for many" (Mt 20:26-28). With these words Jesus rejects the view of secular authority and replaces it with a sacred, servant authority. Of "lording over" and "exercising authority over" people, Jesus says this is not to be so among us. Notice that this is also the concern of Christ's apostles (1 Pet 5:3; 2 Cor 1:24). Absolute authority, the right to command our compliance, is God's alone. This absolute authority has been given to Christ by the Father (Mt 28:18; Heb 1). It does not originate in the church, nor in tradition, nor in the church's leadership. It rests with Jesus Christ who alone is the "head of the body" (Col 1:18; Eph 1:22). But how is it that Christ's authority is communicated to us today? Evangelicals maintain that it comes through the external witness of Holy Scripture and the internal witness of the Holy Spirit.

Contrary to what we would like to believe, elders, pastors and deacons are not in a chain of command, a hierarchical pyramid, which puts them under Christ and over the church. The leaders of a biblical church are simply members of the body of Christ, not an elite oligarchy. They are members whom God has chosen to endow with certain charisms. They are not so much chosen by people as they are recognized because of their character and giftedness. The task of the leaders in the church then is not to run the church, but to determine how the Lord as head wishes the church to proceed. They are to clear the ground in order that the Spirit and the Word might have their way. This demands that they know God's Word and are attuned to his Spirit.

This does not mean guidance is the exclusive prerogative of the leaders. As Acts 15 reveals, there is room for elders and the people to come together and share regarding God's guidance for the church. They will have one common objective, to hear Christ's word for them. If they are in tune with Scripture and with the Holy Spirit, they will hear that word in unanimity. However, there will be times when certain scriptural teachings are not popular with people, and

85

they will want to resist. There will also be times when the guidance or direction given is not palatable to some. In such instances the leaders are not engaged in a power play but seeking to submit to the authority of Christ's headship as it comes through his Word and his Spirit. Any call to submit to church leaders is only a call to submit to their faithfulness to Scripture and to the genuine leading of the Holy Spirit (Heb 13:17; 1 Pet 5:1-5). The call to submission is not carte blanche.

To be a leader in the church, therefore, means that you have become a servant of the Word of God and a conduit of the Spirit of God (1 Cor 4:1-2). This is servant authority, not imposing our own wishes, but serving the Word and the Spirit within the church. To be a leader means that we want to serve rather than to be served and to serve without special reverence or recognition. As T. W. Manson has said, "In the kingdom of God, service is not a stepping stone to nobility, it is nobility, the only kind of nobility that is recognized."[2]

Over or Among?

Several years ago I attended a conference with a group of pastors in which we analyzed two views of authority. We developed the following chart contrasting secular authority with servant authority:

Secular Authority "Lord Over"	Servant Authority "Servant Among"
power base	love/obedience base
gives orders	under orders
unwilling to fail	unafraid/model of transformation
absolutely necessary	expendable
drives like a cowboy	leads like a shepherd
needs strength to subject	finds strength in submission
authoritarian	steward of authority
has gold, makes rules	follows golden rule
seeks personal advancement	seeks to please master
expects to be served	expects to serve

Secular authority demands that one operate from a base of power. Servant authority is not concerned with the issue of power but is concerned with love and obedience. Secular authority wants to give all the orders while those in servant authority see themselves as under orders. Secular leaders fear failure lest they lose their grip of authority over people. Yet servants are unafraid to fail. They are prepared to be a model of those who repent of their failure and rely upon the grace of God to make their inadequacy adequate. As Paul says in 2 Corinthians 3:15-18, we believe that when we turn to the Lord the veil is taken away so that we can behold the glory of the Lord. Rather than concentrating on our failure we are able to concentrate on our transformation as he changes us into his own image.

Secular leaders see themselves as indispensable. But servants model themselves after John the Baptist and see their whole ministry as giving way to another. Secular leaders push and drive their people like cowboys punching cattle, but servants lead like shepherds. Secular leaders need strength in order to keep people in subjection. Servants have recognized that strength comes in submission, that the sign of the Spirit-filled man or woman is submission (Eph 5:18-21).

Secularists are authoritarian while servants are stewards of authority. Secular leaders have all the gold, therefore they can make all the rules; but servants live by the decree of the Lord Jesus that we should do unto others as we would have them do unto us (Mt 7:12). Secular leaders work for their own personal advancement and pleasure, while servants work for the pleasure of their master. And last, secularists expect to be served rather than coming to serve. Disciples of Jesus Christ have signed on as members of the Holy Order of the Towel. They have come to serve. They expect nothing more than that.

Serve like the Son of Man

Isaiah the prophet, writing some seven hundred years before the birth of Christ, predicted in his "servant songs" that the Messiah would not only be the reigning king but also the suffering servant. These servant songs not only tell us about our Lord, but they also picture the kind of leadership we need in the local church.[3] Several characteristics are worthy of note.

1. Servants do not need to advertise themselves (Is 42:2). Jesus did not need advance men or glossy brochures to herald his good works. He quietly went about doing good and let the works speak for themselves.

2. Servants need a profound respect for personality. "A bruised reed he will not break, and a dimly burning wick he will not quench" (Is 42:3). Servants come as encouragers to the weak. They do not crush or condemn, but encourage and lift up.

3. Servants persevere. "He will not fail or be discouraged till he has established justice in the earth; and the coastlands wait for his law" (Is 42:4). Though there is no glory or instant success, they continue to serve without reward.

4. Servants know that their ultimate reward for service is found in their relationship to God. "But I said, 'I have labored in vain, I have spent my strength for nothing and vanity; yet surely my right is with the LORD, and my recompense with my God" (Is 49:4). There is no glory in being a servant. Servants are often discouraged and frustrated, yet they remember that their reward is from God and with that they are content.

5. Servants are teachable. "The Lord GOD has given me the tongue of those who are taught, that I may know how to sustain with a word him that is weary. Morning by morning he wakens, he wakens my ear to hear as those who are taught. The Lord GOD has opened my ear, and I was not

rebellious, I turned not backward" (Is 50:4-5). Daily servants listen and heed God's Word. The nourishment they receive will not be for their benefit alone but for the enrichment of others as they attempt to sustain those who are weary and downtrodden.

6. Servants are vulnerable. "I gave my back to the smiters, and my cheeks to those who pulled out the beard; I hid not my face from shame and spitting" (Is 50:6). Servants are not free of hurt or humiliation. They can heal in part because they themselves have been wounded.

7. Servants are secure. "For the Lord GOD helps me; therefore I have not been confounded; therefore I have set my face like a flint, and I know that I shall not be put to shame; he who vindicates me is near. Who will contend with me? . . . Behold, the Lord GOD helps me; who will declare me guilty?" (Is 50:7-9). Though abused and torn, servants are confident that God will not fail or depart from them.

8. Servants will be exhalted because they have been humiliated. "Behold, my servant shall prosper, he shall be exalted and lifted up, and shall be very high" (Is 52:13). The path of servanthood leads upward to the plain of victory. Victory may come only in our future reign with Christ, but even this is not too long to wait.

9. Servants are prepared to be rejected in order to serve. "But he was wounded for our transgressions, he was bruised for our iniquities; upon him was the chastisement that made us whole, and with his stripes we are healed (Is 53:5). There will be times when leadership is rejected. That will test the leader, but rejection is a part of his portfolio. Even rejection may serve God's purposes.

In addressing our congregation one morning, Dr. Stanley Mooneyham, the director of World Vision International, suggested that Jesus' call was not only for involvement, but for identification. Involvement for Christ is not enough, unless we also identify with him. The motif of the suffering servant should then characterize not only our personal behavior but our life together. It is only in this context that we can identify with a suffering world and minister like a servant.

"So That's What It Looks Like!"

Two pictures of servanthood in my recent experience have been worth more than a thousand books on the subject. The first I saw one evening at a communion service at St. Michael's Le Belfrey, York, England. My wife and I had been in the country for several weeks and had been guests of St. Michael's. The service began with music and dance as the congregation was led in worship. Following this, the rector, David Watson, preached for about thirty minutes. Anywhere else this might have seemed the time to disband, but not at St. Michael's. We then began preparation for the Eucharist with more singing and praise. Then the elders came forward. Some served the bread and wine as parishioners came forward. Others went to the kneeling rail and ministered to those who wanted prayer and counseling. For over an hour people came forward to these shepherds, sharing their deepest needs and going away refreshed. Sitting in the middle section of the church, I watched with open mouth as these brothers poured out Christ's concern for his sheep. No other statement or book has affected me as profoundly as that picture—loving shepherds, listening and pouring out affection to God's people; servants, bringing the presence of God's Word and Spirit; sufferers, prepared to enter the pain of parishioners; simple men, humble men, bringing the fragrance of Christ to his people.

The second picture is widely recognized—the Nobel Peace Prize winner Mother Theresa of Calcutta. In 1977 Mother Theresa came to our city to speak to the United Nations Conference on World Habitation. On entering the crowded auditorium, she received a ten-minute standing ovation. That day she served our community as a servant of the Word and conduit of the Holy Spirit. What impresses people about Mother Theresa is not her oratory skills but her commitment to aid those who are suffering and dying, not for any recognition she might receive but for the pleasure of serving her master. I recently read a book which mentioned Mother Theresa in just one sentence. It simply said, "Mother Theresa of Calcutta still cleans out the toilets in her community."[4] It is certainly this kind of servant attitude which Jesus referred to when he said, "whoever wishes to be first among you shall be your slave."

During my weekly routine I often catch myself saying, "You shouldn't be doing this job! Your gifts are in teaching and preaching, not in folding chairs and mopping floors." But this is my secular man, responding to his view of authority. He demands that I get on top and stay there. He encourages me to do only jobs befitting the dignity of my position. He aids me to rationalize that if I do this job someone else will lose the privilege of serving. But I believe I have now come to the bottom of his lie. It all rests in my pride—pride which resists serving and waits to be served, arrogance which sees others as inferior and therefore better suited for such menial tasks.

But, thanks be to God, I have seen the shepherds of St. Michael's and the servant of Calcutta, and most of all the suffering servant of Calvary. Each of them beckons the Spirit of God within me to confess that "it shall not be so among you" and that only by serving will we be leading.

Sola Pastora or Plural Leadership?

6

Bud Wilkinson, former football coach for the University of Oklahoma, was once asked by a television reporter what contribution modern football had made to physical fitness. His reply was, "Absolutely nothing." He went on, "I define football as twenty-two men on the field who desperately need rest and fifty thousand people in the grandstand who desperately need exercise."[1] Regrettably, the church is often in the same predicament—one or two people desperately in need of rest surrounded by five hundred to a thousand people who desperately need exercise. From a faulty view of leadership we develop a faulty view of the laity. The average church in North America runs on the initiative of one or two professionals who orchestrate a host of spectators. But when Jesus Christ inaugurated his church at Pentecost, he had no intention of developing a spiritual welfare society. He did not call people to be spiritually unemployed, but to serve as his priests. Therefore the frozen assets of the church must be thawed and set to work. Every believer must sense that he or she is useful and has ministry in the body of Christ.

Leaders can do much to encourage full participation in the priesthood of all believers. But some church leaders seem to have added a new doctrine to the Reformation statements of by grace alone, by faith alone and by Scripture alone. We could call it "sola pastora," by the pastor alone. Ray Stedman, pastor of Peninsula Bible Church in Palo Alto, California, has been roasted a number of occasions for suggesting that "some evangelicals have substituted for one Pope over the church, a pope in every church" —the superstar pastor who runs and controls the church as though he were the director of a large corporation. Such a picture is foreign to the New Testament. It may not be foreign to church history, but it is to the New Testament.

The blame should not be placed exclusively on the pastor. In many congregations this role is foisted on the leader, "That's what we pay him for." But pastors of a church are not employees of the church, they are honored servants who have been set apart and given time in which to see the ministry accomplished. Nevertheless, they are not called to do this alone. Ephesians 4:11-16 makes it quite clear that pastoral gifts are for equipping and facilitating the saints to minister. The whole body is able to make use of its gifts as it is equipped and set free by its leaders. Leaders are player-coaches. Sometimes they play, but most of the time they coach. Their goal is to see the entire body mature in their gifts. Only then will the church be a fully equipped priesthood and the leaders be functioning in their God-given positions.

Collegial Leadership
One way of encouraging the participation of the entire body is for there to be plurality in the leadership itself. In fact, the New Testament teaches this principle. Paul advised Titus to appoint elders in every local church (Tit 1:5). During the first century there were three levels of

leadership in the church. First, there were those who had authority over all the church and had ministry in those churches: apostles. Second, there were those who had gifts of evangelism and prophecy and were led by the Holy Spirit to go from city to city exercising their ministry: evangelists and prophets. Third, there were those who exercised residential gifts: pastors and teachers. In the context of residential ministry there were three specific words used for local leadership. At first these terms appear to be hierarchical in their development: a closer examination, however, will reveal that they are interchangeable in their usage. They describe the collegial leadership of the local congregation.

The term *elder* originates in the Jewish synagogue and describes a mature man. In 1 Timothy 5 the term can either apply to an older man (vs. 1) or to the function of an elder (vs. 17). When applied to the New Testament function, the word usually appears in the plural (Acts 11:30; 14:23; 15:2; 16:4; 20:17; 1 Tim 5:17; Tit 1:5; Jas 5:14; 1 Pet 5:1). A plurality of elders is seen as a necessary safeguard to a one-man rule of the church, a Diatrophes-syndrome (3 Jn).

It is clear that some of those designated elders were financially supported by the church (1 Tim 5:17). Their double honor was respect and material assistance. However, not all elders were remunerated in such fashion. This in no sense made them any less a part of the eldership. Because those elders who teach and preach must have the necessary time for study and preparation, the church consented to allow them to have this time by supporting them financially. In no sense does this verse teach us a clergy-laity distinction. It was not until the time of Origen in the third century that *the clergy* became an established term for those who held office in the church. But such a distinction has no place in Paul's communication to Timothy or Titus.

Though the popular use of the word *bishop* leads us to think in hierarchical terms, the New Testament seems not to use the term in this way. *Bishop* or *Overseer* describes the duty of an elder. He is an onlooker, an observer, a protector (Acts 20:28; 1 Tim 3:1; 1 Pet 2:25).

The third word, *pastor,* describes the ministry of elders in figurative terms as those who shepherd sheep (Jn 10:1-18; Eph 4:11; Heb 13:20; 1 Pet 2:25). Again, these three terms are used interchangeably to describe leaders of local churches (Acts 20:17, 28; Tit 1:5, 7; 1 Pet 5:1-2).

The question might well be asked, If eldership is a spiritual gift, why is it not mentioned in 1 Corinthians 12 or Romans 12, along with the other spiritual gifts? The answer is that these gifts are mentioned, yet the terminology is quite flexible. In 1 Corinthians 12:28 the term *administrators* is used for this particular gift. In Romans 12:8 (NASB or NIV) and 1 Thessalonians 5:12 the spiritual gift is defined as leading. All of this underscores the great flexibility in the descriptions and functions of those who exercised leadership in the early church. Howard Snyder rightly concludes:

> The important teachings from the New Testament are: (1) God provided the necessary leaders, (2) this leadership was seen in terms of the exercise of spiritual gifts, and (3) there was great flexibility and fluidity in the way these leadership functions operated and were understood in the early church.[2]

Eldership Begins with Character

Paul stresses character when he lists the qualifications of elders in a local church. He does not assume that secular standards of success necessarily transfer into the church. Just because someone is able to lead a large business or to teach in a university does not necessarily mean that he or she is qualified to shepherd and teach the people of God. Leadership within the church is a spiritual gift and is marked by an impeccable character.

In 1 Timothy 3, Paul lists the essential characteristics of an elder. A question that is immediately addressed is whether or not it is right for a person to aspire to be an elder (3:1). In the worst sense of the word *aspire,* we might think of a man longing to be the big cheese. The word is sometimes used in a negative context (1 Tim 6:10), but here it is used in a good sense. And what Paul says comes as encouragement to those with a general reluctance for assuming oversight responsibility.

There were and are at least three good reasons for being reluctant to assume the responsibility of an elder. First, there is the sacrifice of carrying the emotional load of the church. Paul knew well the daily pressure of caring for the church (2 Cor 11:28). Second, there may be reluctance because one's life is on the line. In every generation persecution and martyrdom begins with the leaders of the church. In the violent period of the first century, leaders necessarily faced the loss of their own lives in accepting this ministry. Third, there is a reluctance because of the time commitment. While others are able to spend free time in holidays, hobbies and making extra money, elders are called to sacrifice much of this time to minister to the flock. I recently heard of an elder who turned down an invitation to a presidential dinner at the White House because his eldership responsibilities did not allow him to have the evening free.

Beginning in verse 2, Paul gives a list of things that ought to characterize an overseer. First, he is to be above reproach. This seems to be an all-embracing description of an elder. *Above reproach* does not mean unapproachable, but rather irreproachable in behavior. You should not be able to find fault with him.

An elder should be the husband of one wife. This is somewhat more difficult than it appears at first. Is Paul forbidding bigamy or polygamy? I doubt it. These practices were already frowned upon in Judaism, and it's questionable that either would even need to be mentioned as a qualification for a Christian leader. Later in church history it was suggested that if an elder's wife died or he was divorced for some biblical reason he should not remarry.[3] Remarriage was viewed as self-indulgence and celibacy as meritorious. However, it appears that Scripture maintains the right of remarriage for those whose marriage has been terminated according to biblical justification (Rom 7:1-3). The best interpretation is to see this qualification as a demand for strict marital fidelity—emotional and sexual fidelity to one wife at a time. An elder is to be a one-woman man.

Some will doubtlessly ask at this point, Is an elder to be the wife of one husband? It is not my intention to defend or refute female eldership in the church. For those who have such a practice, then all of the qualifications apply equally to women as well as to men.

Elders are to be temperate. This does not have anything to do with alcohol; that comes later. As Paul uses the term (1 Thess 5:6, 8) it refers to being sober and clear-headed, awake to what is going on in one's own life, family and church fellowship. Elders should not be drowsy sleepers who go through life unaware of the conflict in establishing Christ's kingdom.

Elders are to be prudent. They are to exercise self-control. Elders should control their tongues, their time, their temper and their own devotional life (1 Tim 4:7-8).

Elders are to be respectable. They are to carry about a certain sense of dignity or properness. This does not at all mean that they should be snobbish or conceited, but that they be honorable and orderly in all things.

Elders are to be hospitable. The Greek word for hospitality literally means "lover of strangers." Hospitality is not primarily concerned with swapping meals with other members of the church, but rather with welcoming overnight guests and ministering to those who are homeless. As Karen Mains points out, hospitality is found in the dictionary between *hospice,* a place for strangers, and *hospital,* a place for those needing care.[4]

Elders should be able to teach. They should know correct doctrine and be able to communicate it. This does not mean that all elders must be preachers. There are other avenues for teaching such as one-to-one discipling, small groups and classes. However, in any group of elders there ought to be two or three who equip themselves for public preaching and teaching. The practice of having only one preacher/teacher per congregation, and that one being a professional, sorely misses the New Testament perspective.

Elders should not be addicted to wine. The imagery here is of one who sits all day long at the wine table. The requirement is not that elders must be abstainers or teetotalers. However, they must abstain from drunkenness.

Elders should not be pugnacious, but rather gentle and uncontentious. They are not to be disposed toward violence and brutality, but rather to be gentle, yielding and kind. They should not be pushy, but rather peaceable. This is probably one of the greatest assets that elders can have. They realize that there is too much work to be done to waste time fighting with one another.

Elders should be free from the love of money. Covetousness cannot be tolerated among those designated as elders. Paul is clear that the love of money is the root of all sorts of evil and some by longing for it have wandered away from the faith (1 Tim 6:10). He is also aware that the sins of some persons are quite evident, disqualifying them from eldership, but others' sins are not so evident. Therefore elders are to take a long hard look at any new candidate for this role (1 Tim 5:22, 24-25).

Elders should not be new converts (1 Tim 3:6-7). Irrespective of social rank or affluence, new converts are too young in the faith to be made overseers of the community. Such a prohibition eliminates the conceit which easily comes from an inflated self-importance, a trap door for the devil's work.

Elders are to have a good reputation with those outside the church. This is much harder than one would suspect, for elders in their secular vocation are called to be different. As salt and light they may often be brought into conflict with those with whom they work. But even their coworkers should be able to testify that their behavior is above reproach.

Elders are to have children who believe (Tit 1:6). I doubt that this means each minor, eighteen and under, must have made a profession of faith, but I do think it implies that the children of elders are cooperating with their spiritual leadership.

Family tutorship is the preparation ground for leadership in a church (1 Tim 3:4-5). The church is really the family writ large. This does not necessarily disqualify single people from exercising the gift and function of an elder. But it does suggest that the majority of elders should be rooted in a nuclear family. Elders must be able to manage their own households well. As I pointed out earlier, *manage* (proistēmi) is the same word used in Romans 12:8 and 1 Thessalonians 5:12 as the gift of leading. Elders are able to keep their children under control with all dignity. The dignity refers to the action of the elders and not the children.[5] With the proper physical leverage and verbal assault a parent can keep almost any child in line. But that type of behavior would be unbecoming to an elder.

I recently had an opportunity to grow in this area with my three-year-old son. Having played hard at a weekend conference, he fell asleep on the way home. At dinner time

I was forced to wake him. Carrying this sleepy little baggage into the restaurant, I wondered what kind of explosion we were in for. Lying in my lap in the booth, he appeared most uncooperative. For the next twenty minutes we did a dance together. He was testing me to see whether or not I would become loud, abusive or violent to get him to eat his meal. I knew that the little guy was just testing me and that it was also a learning experience for the sermon I was to preach the next Sunday. The test was to see him awake and eating his pizza without shrieks of anger or crying. Lovingly and gently I attempted to nurture his sleepy head back to life. I was ever so thankful when he consented to eat his dinner with the rest of us. The test was over. I had won on both counts. He was eating his meal, and it had been accomplished without a verbal or physical explosion.

Paul makes use of two metaphors in this section. First is the managerial aspect wc have just looked at, and then there is a medical metaphor. The Greek word for "to take care" *(epimeleomai)* is only used twice in the New Testament, here and in the story of the Good Samaritan. The Samaritan, when he saw the man who had fallen among the robbers, "had compassion, and went to him and bound up his wounds, pouring on oil and wine; then he set him on his own beast and brought him to an inn, and took care of him. And the next day he took out two denarii and gave them to the innkeeper, saying, 'Take care of him; and whatever more you spend, I will repay you when I come back' " (Lk 10:33-35).

Leadership in the church begins in our homes with our ability to see and feel compassion for those who are hurting in our own families. It is easy in the rush of ministry to pass over the obvious needs of our own wives and children. All too often, I fear, we are taught: "There is no greater love than this, that an elder would lay down his wife for the ministry."

Good elders, however, are catechized by bandaging the wounds of their own spouses and children, hearing their hurts and their struggles for adulthood. Proper discipline in this area may mean stepping back from activities which give me a sense of fulfillment and meaning in order that my children and spouse might take a greater place. Elders need to consider themselves Good Samaritans to their own family. Elders cannot determine or control the choices of their spouses or children. But they can control their own choices as to the amount and quality of time they spend with their families.

I need not recount the stories of those who have chosen to win the world at the expense of their families. The Spirit of God is calling elders to give priority to their families. We should never forget that model husbands and wives are always smaller than the real thing. We all have need of improvement. Again, it cannot be stressed enough that the quality of the elders' homelives will affect the quality of the local church. Elders will likely do with the church what they do with their families. If their family lives are successful, then their church will likely be successful. If there are some major flaws in their family lives, then these flaws will likely manifest themselves in the church.

The Appointment Process
Paul's injunctions to Timothy and Titus, as well as his own example in Acts 14:23, suggest that the appointment of elders is a significant feature of any church's life. Each church will probably go about the appointment of its leaders in a somewhat different fashion. In some church governments, the congregation is asked to make suggestions regarding possible leaders. From this a slate is drawn for people to vote upon. In other traditions the slate is actually drawn up by the present leadership and the congregation votes.

Each of these alternatives has something to commend it but also fails at certain points. The church needs to be careful that it is not adopting a secular standard for evaluating leaders and appointing leaders. I once heard F. F. Bruce say that churches more often than not adopt the political standards of the societies in which they serve rather than biblical standards. Therefore, in highly authoritarian governments, church appointments are usually made unilaterally and without the discussion of the congregation. In democratic structures everyone expects his vote and say. In each case the church must steer a middle course, for it is neither a democracy nor an oligarchy. The following five steps have been helpful to our own community in the recognition and appointment of elders.

1. First, there is recognition of a person's gift of eldership. Eldership is something for which one is gifted. As Paul said to the Ephesian elders, "The Holy Spirit has made you overseers, to care for the church of God" (Acts 20:28). Therefore the process of appointing elders is not so much the choosing of elders but recognizing those whom the Holy Spirit has already appointed. The additional question of whether or not the person meets the qualifications of 1 Timothy 3 is also asked. This procedure is undertaken by the presiding elders. They are most aware of the demands of an elder and the qualities that are essential.

2. The present elders then approach those whose gifts have been recognized and ask them and their families whether or not they desire to function as elders in the community (1 Tim 3:1). Are they prepared to make the time commitments that such a job will demand? Are they prepared to carry the emotional burden of the fellowship? If there is any hesitation on the part of their spouses or children, then the elders counsel them not to assume this responsibility. This is a family decision and will demand family unanimity.

3. The council of elders (or presbytery) then waits for an acceptance or rejection of the invitation to join the elders. The elders have the confidence that God has set this person aside for eldership, but there must be confirmation by that person. Usually this reflection time takes from four to six weeks. If the person says yes to the ministry of eldership, then we move to stage four.

4. At this point the elders come before the congregation with their findings. They suggest that this person has the gifts and calling of an elder. They relay the person's desire and acceptance of this responsibility. Now comes the final step in the appointment. There must be confirmation by the congregation that this person qualifies and is being set apart by the Holy Spirit. Some will suggest that the best way to determine this factor is to vote. But voting should not be used as a selection procedure. Rather it should serve to confirm the decision of the elders. In our own community we do not vote. Rather we give a period of four weeks during which people are encouraged to share with the elders either their affirmation or reservations regarding such appointments. The elders believe that this is a process where the Holy Spirit must communicate his mind to the congregation as well as to the elders. Because the Holy Spirit has one mind, we believe that we shall come to a common agreement regarding the appointment. If there are hesitations by members of the body, strong hesitations, then the elders do not make that appointment. Each elder must carry the respect of the community. If that respect is not already present, it will not be gained by assuming the role of an elder.

5. Once those invited have accepted their call to be elders and been confirmed by the community, they are then commissioned in the presence of the congregation. This gives the Christian community an opportunity to associate particular faces with the injunction to "obey your

leaders and submit to them; for they are keeping watch over your souls, as men who will have to give account" (Heb 13:17).

No doubt to some this whole procedure appears to grant too much authority to the present leaders. But this is not unchecked authority. These appointments must pass through four checkpoints before approval. The elders must see the gift, the person and his family must be willing to assume the responsibility, then the person must accept the invitation and receive the confirmation of the community. All of these checks allow the Holy Spirit to speak his mind regarding the appointment.

Elders for Life?

And for how long is an elder appointed? Some would suggest only for a specified period of time. I would suggest, however, that the appointment by the Holy Spirit is a gift for life. This does not mean that elders cannot be removed from office or that they are immune from evaluation. Guidelines must be developed for the removal or refreshment of elders who are failing in their positions. The following are helpful.

Elders might legitimately be removed from the presbytery if they move outside the natural geographical boundaries of the community. Similarly, they might be removed if they are absent from the presbytery for more than six months without the permission of the other elders. Serious immoral behavior would also constitute cause for removal.

According to 1 Timothy 5:19 any accusation against an elder regarding his behavior should be confirmed by two or three witnesses. Repentance and forgiveness are sufficient to restore a sinning elder just as they are for any other believer. If the severity of the sinful behavior has destroyed the confidence of the congregation in this person, then the presbytery may find it necessary to encourage the person to step down. This does not mean that he cannot be reappointed to the office later on.

Although elders have been gifted by the Holy Spirit for such ministry, they can quench or grieve those gifts. Therefore, every two years elders ought to review their ministries with one another. In such an environment candid discussion must take place regarding the fruitfulness and faithfulness of one another's ministry. During this time an elder can evaluate his own performance. With his fellow elders he will then either feel confirmed to stay in the ministry of eldership or will find himself directed not to assume that position any longer.

Occasionally elders are not so much stifling their gifts as they are simply worn out. Therefore every church should have a policy of an elder sabbatical. Every fourth to seventh year an elder should be relieved of his responsibilities. The elder can then hand over his portfolios and take a twelve-month break. At the end of that time he will return to the presbytery and take on appropriate duties.

Another question that is often raised is, How many elders ought to be appointed? The answer to that is not necessarily fixed in stone. A general rule is that as many elders as are necessary to fulfill the shepherding mandate of the congregation ought to be appointed. In practical terms, one person cannot shepherd more than a few dozen people. Some growing communities suggest at least one elder for every ten families. Obviously with a growing church, this means that someone is spending a great deal of time training and equipping new elders for their calling. However, one caution should be voiced. An eldership which reaches into twenty and thirty often falls into the trap of simply being a board of directors. It is essential that elders have the same kind of relationship with one another that they are to have with their own sheep. Therefore to some degree the numbers must be manageable and personal.

Give Up Your Small Ambitions

Will Rogers once said that the history of North America would be written in three phases: the passing of the Indian, the passing of the buffalo and the passing of the buck. As those who believe that God is alive and speaking to his church today, elders are not hesitant to stop passing the buck by going to him when it's time to make a decision. It is crucial that the elders' meetings be rid of secular mindsets. They are not board meetings, but meetings of fellow members of the body of Christ who have come to listen to the mind of the Holy Spirit. All the elders should be prepared to give up their small ambitions for the future of the church and to seek together instead to know the mind of Christ. They should want to pray repeatedly through the meeting with one another and to read Scripture which reminds them of their heavenly calling and the spiritual nature of the process in which they are involved. This does not mean that they should be sloppy or disorderly. But the goal is to be *orderly,* not necessarily *businesslike.*

At our meetings we have a prepared agenda, but we do not have prepared resolutions. The resolutions are for the Holy Spirit as he speaks to the corporate body gathered together. As we move through the agenda there is full discussion of all of the issues, each elder making his contribution as we go. There are times when everyone's dander is raised. The mark of the Spirit's presence is not the absence of argument, but the quality of the argument. Good argument involves discussion which derives from loyalty to one another. We believe the best of one another. We believe that every person gathered in the room desires one thing above all else and that is to know Christ's mind. We realize that we are married to one another and that divorce is not possible. Therefore we shall never leave angry or heated with one another, for that only indicates that we have not been controlled by Christ's Spirit.

As we discuss with one another and make comments, each elder is listening for that word from the Holy Spirit with which each of us can agree. As elders we are committed to unanimous decision making. Every elder must agree or no action will be taken. Some of you may be asking, How then can any action take place? Again it is possible because each of us brings not his own agenda but desires to hear what the Spirit is saying to the church. Submission to the Holy Spirit of God will also lead us to be submissive to one another. Yes, we are prepared to bend and be flexible in response to anything that God says to us. We make mistakes in our decisions from time to time and seek to learn from them. As it is said, good judgment comes from experience, and experience comes from bad judgment. But the more elders come together with one concern, to know Christ's mind, and the more they are committed to be loyal to one another and submit to one another and learn from their own mistakes, God will certainly give abundant grace to their decision making. There is no greater joy than to sit with a group of elders for two or three hours and then have the Holy Spirit reveal through the word of one the decision that ought to be made, a decision which bears witness with all of our hearts that God has clearly led us.

The Trouble with the World

A major British newspaper once requested its readers to respond to the question, "What's wrong with the world today?" The literary giant, G. K. Chesterton, responded as follows:

Dear Sirs:

I am.

Sincerely yours, G. K. Chesterton

It's about time that we as church leaders admit that we are a major problem in the church. Much of our leadership has been too dominant or too distant. We have failed to recognize the servant authority that is to characterize our ministry. We have too easily jettisoned the biblical criteria and substituted for it our own standards. We must acknowledge that in many of our churches the entire ministry has been relegated to the solo professional. We have fought congregational battles as each person voted for their own agenda and had no idea of what the Spirit was saying. We have let our traditions and pragmatic considerations determine the way we appoint leaders, rather than appealing to apostolic procedures. We have failed by letting covetous men and women sit on our boards, by letting those with secular credentials pass as spiritual people and by accepting a sixty-per-cent vote as the leading of the Holy Spirit. The church will not rise beyond the level of its leadership. Malachi's refining fire must first visit us before we can expect a new revitalization of the church.

Fifty
Ways to
Leave
Your Lover
7

You just slip out the back, Jack
Make a new plan, Stan
You don't need to be coy, Roy
Just get yourself free
Hop on the bus, Gus
You don't need to discuss much
Just drop off the key, Lee
And get yourself free[1]

The first time I heard Paul Simon's "Fifty Ways to Leave Your Lover" was just moments after listening to a radio program on twenty-five-dollar instant divorce. Here again I was being seduced into believing a marital nightmare could be ended by a blissful separation. "Don't make no fuss, just get on the bus." As the music continued, I began to realize how easy it is for the seed of divorce to be sown in the unreflective consciences, even of Christians in stable marriages. No wonder Malachi warns us to take heed to ourselves (2:15), lest we should find ourselves betraying the spouse of our youth.

Divorce statistics have a way of dulling our responses to

the tragedy of marital failure. In Canada when the divorce rate moved from one out of four to one out of three, we felt no appreciable difference. But translated into personal terms, the increase means greater emotional pain, awkward social readjustments, and an affixed financial and legal burden on the state. Living in a neighborhood where forty per cent of all real estate sales are due to broken homes, I readily recognize the truth of the conclusion of a *Time* essay on divorce: "Divorce is always a tragedy, no matter how civilized the handling of it, it is always a confession of human failure, even when it is the sorry better of sorry alternatives."[2]

No one benefits in divorce, everyones loses. For an adult, divorce is akin to the death of a spouse. Grief and resentment follow in the wake of disengagement. But children are the greatest losers.[3] I once heard the head of a children's psychiatric unit describe the trauma in this manner: "For a child, divorce is the explosion of his world. It is equivalent to the devastating effects of Hiroshima or Nagasaki. The scale is different, but the impact is similar."

We must also ask what the implications of increased divorce are for society. Is it not tearing the very fabric of our culture? Ask a schoolteacher who must discipline the chaos of a classroom where over one-half the children come from single-parent families. Ask local law enforcement officials about the correlation between marital failure and juvenile crime. Ask local and state representatives about the amount of tax revenues spent yearly for broken families.

In my own country, Canada, there are hundreds of social services available to those suffering the fallout of marital failure: free legal aid, welfare benefits for the spouse who stays at home to watch young children, subsidized day-care services, and psychiatric counseling for those suffering the emotional pain of separation. All of these humanitarian efforts are to be genuinely applauded. However, we must ask pragmatically, How long can we go on spending on these programs before financial bankruptcy finally overtakes us?

All Looks Yellow from a Jaundiced Eye

Sir Winston Churchill once defined a fanatic as one "who could not change his mind and would not change the subject." I must confess, by that definition, I have become a fanatic. One can only tolerate so long the countless number of evangelical leaders who are presently divorced yet still functioning within the structure of the Christian community. I want to make clear from the start that I know every marital failure is unique and cannot be placed into a generalized category. There are biblical grounds for divorce, and innocent parties (a term I use cautiously) should not be tarred with the same brush as the guilty. Even for the guilty, forgiveness and reconciliation within the church are available. The church has been generally slow in responding to penitents in this area; in its more thoughtful moments it has wished not to be mediators of cheap grace. However, in our reluctance we have often given the impression that divorce is unforgivable or that forgiveness must be merited before it can be conferred. Both ideas are contrary to the spirit and content of the gospel. Thankfully, there are signs that the church is beginning to come to grips with this difficult pastoral problem.

What concerns me, though, is how lightly divorce is often taken. A person gets divorced and continues to carry on a public ministry as though nothing significant had really happened. But something has happened. It matters not whether you are clergyman or layman, God hates divorce and those who attempt to cover up the gravity of their actions.

Before we look at several Old and New Testament pas-

113

sages on divorce and remarriage, we need to agree on at least one presupposition, since where you stand makes a difference in what you see and how you behave. Though the state may permit divorce for various reasons (for example, leprosy, vagrancy, incompatibility; mental cruelty, etc.), though our culture may condone and encourage us to choose this option ("you can't please everybody, so you might as well please yourself"), and though everything in our reason and emotion cries out for this solution, Christians are bound to a different loyalty. Our loyalty is to the kingdom rule of Christ, not Caesar. Our lives are governed by Scripture, not culture. And when we feel alone and confused by our own emotions, we are given God's precious gifts of the Holy Spirit and the church to come alongside and aid us in carrying out Christ's word. Jesus is Lord, not just of our salvation, but also of weak and fragile marriages.

Regulation, Not Encouragement: Deuteronomy 24:1-4

In examining the Mosaic legislation on divorce (Deut 24:1-4), we must be careful to discern its intent. First of all, it says nothing about the divine approval or the moral legitimacy of divorce. It is a description of the procedures to be followed when divorce occurs. It does not institute divorce, for it treats it as a practice already known, whether by custom or some other legislation. It neither enjoins or encourages it, but rather regulates it.

That regulation is twofold. First, it calls for the granting of a certificate of divorce. This action was meant to halt the hasty divorce which springs from a thoughtless and emotive argument. "Get out of my house and don't ever come back." Under this legislation there was to be reflection and sobriety in one's action. The certificate itself also provided the woman, since women could not divorce men, with legal protection. She had a legal document which stated her release from the previous marriage and the freedom to marry again without any accusation of adultery. The bill itself appeared in a form similar to this:

On _____ day of the week _____ day of the month _____ in the year _____ I who am also called son of _____ of the city of _____ by the river of _____ do hereby consent with my own will, being under no restraint, and I do hereby release, send away, and put aside thee, my wife _____ who is also called daughter of _____ who is this day in the city of _____ by the river of _____ who have been my wife for some time past; and thus I do release thee, and send thee away and put thee aside that thou mayest have permission and control over thyself to go to be married to any man that thou mayest desire; and that no man shall hinder thee from this day forward, and thou art permitted to any man, and this shall be unto thee from me a bill of dismissal, a document of release, and a letter of freedom, according to the law of Moses and Israel.

_____ the son of _____ Witness

_____ the son of _____ Witness[4]

The second element of the regulation, and grammatically the major intent of the legislation, is to forbid the remarriage of divorced persons to their original spouses. This is called an abomination before the Lord because in practical terms it is adultery. It is cohabiting with a person other than your spouse, then returning to your original marriage partner.

When Jesus comments on this section of the Mosaic law, he reminds his listeners that these procedures were only permitted because of the hardness of the human heart (Mt 19:8). Divorce would continue because we are covenant breakers, but divorce without these regulations would heap on women further abuse and insult. Therefore divorce must be regulated.

I believe this ought to encourage Christians to be concerned about the divorce laws of their province or state. We realize that men and women are sinful and will take unfair advantage if this is not regulated. In one of our Prairie Provinces of Canada, a divorced farmer's wife is suing to overturn a previous court ruling. This woman put in twenty-five years of fifteen-hour-a-day labor. Chores and children consumed her life. But all the money and assets were in her husband's name. The old man gets the itch, sells the farm and retires his wife off to an old folks' home without a cent. He claims the farm and assets are all his; she was only a boarder. But surely she was more than that! Christians want, because we believe God wants, laws which are just in their treatment of both husbands and wives.

Hardness of heart can also be seen in the reason for allowing divorce. The man is permitted to divorce his wife because "he has found some indecency in her." The exact meaning of *indecency* seems to have been as vague in the thirteenth century B.C. as it was in the first century A.D. The word literally means "nakedness of a thing" and refers to something that is impure or improper about one's behavior. However, rabbinical interpreters were divided over its precise meaning. The school of Shammai regarded it as unchastity, while the more liberal school of Hillel saw it as anything displeasing to the husband.[5] Alfred Edersheim, in commenting on some of the frivolous reasons given by the school of Hillel, says that this indecency

> included every kind of impropriety, such as going about with loose hair, spinning in the street, familiarly talking with men, ill-treating her husband's parents in his presence, brawling, that is, speaking to her husband so loudly that the neighbours could hear her in the adjoining house, a generally bad reputation, or the discovery of fraud before marriage.[6]

Most evangelical scholars conclude with John Murray that

the true significance of this word falls somewhere between the very strict view (adultery) and the lax view (for any reason at all). Adultery is rejected because it is handled separately by other Mosaic legislation (Deut 22:22; Lev 20:10), for which the sentence was death for both participants. The lax view is rejected because of its relativistic absurdity and potential for abuse. It seems that the phrase denotes some gross impropriety which arouses the revulsion of the husband to such an extent that the marriage can no longer work. It could refer to a physical deficiency which kept the woman from bearing children, or even some shameful conduct of sexual life which fell short of illicit sexual intercourse. Again, the legislation was not designed to encourage divorce, only to check its indiscriminate use by impatient and ungracious husbands. It was a word that spoke strongly to protect women's rights in a society which viewed them as having none.

Stop Encouraging Divorce: Matthew 19:3-12

Jesus' view of divorce is recorded in Matthew 19:3-12 (cf. Mk 10:1-12). Teaching and healing in Judea beyond the Jordan, Jesus encounters some of the disciples of Rabbi Hillel. They believe that Moses approved of divorce in any marriage which proved inconvenient for the husband. This interpretation was widespread and apparently included many of Jesus' own disciples among its adherents. These Pharisees, seeking to cast Jesus in an unpopular light, asked him if he agreed with this widespread opinion that divorce could be granted for just any cause at all (NIV and NEB catch the flavor of this better than RSV and NASB). Jesus answered with an unequivocal no.

While the Pharisees wanted to talk about divorce, Jesus wanted to discuss marriage. Quoting from Genesis 1 and 2, Jesus discloses God's intention of a permanent, one-flesh association. God has joined husband and wife together and

117

has witnessed their covenant to an enduring shared intimacy. God never intended this covenant to be terminated.

At every stage of married life there are new learning experiences. They are meant to be shared by those who have gone through previous experiences together. The rewards of parenthood are to be followed by the rewards of grandparenthood. Divorce is a short circuit of that experience. Any new beginnings, though they may appear thrilling, are really only a return to a more elementary level of living. Divorce and remarriage is a retrogressive step rather than progressive.

Jesus' rebuke of the Pharisees for their accommodation of easy divorce is sharp and direct, "What therefore God has joined together, let not man put asunder." They reply, "Well, what about Moses, didn't he command it?" No, says Jesus, Moses was regulating an environment which already existed, but from creation it was never intended to be this way.

Martin Luther King once said, "We shall have to repent in this generation, not so much for the evil deeds of the wicked people, but for the appalling silence of the good people." The evangelical church has been appallingly silent on the consequences of divorce. When we have spoken, it has often sounded as though we were only crying wolf. But isn't it now time for Christians to show by solid psychological and sociological data that divorce is rotting the very heart of our nation? That its unchecked progress spells emotional disaster for the next generation? That the encouragement of easy divorce benefits no one?

Matthew is the only Gospel writer to include Jesus' exception clause regarding divorce (Mt 5:32; 19:9; cf. Mk 10:11-12; Lk 16:18). However, we should not jump to the conclusion that we have a scribal interpolation, therefore leading us to reject Matthew's addition. Rather, we should argue for the authentic nature of Matthew's word based on the assumption that Mark and Luke took the exception for granted.

"Except for unchastity" placed a drastic restriction on the interpretation of Hillel. It was a stout rebuke to husbands who had easily disposed of innocent wives. The woman at the well (Jn 4), for example, may not have been so much an immoral woman as the victim of four picky husbands. Jesus says that if you put your wife away for any cause except unchastity and subsequently remarry, you are committing adultery; for the original covenant is still binding.

A great deal of controversy surrounds the meaning of the word *unchastity (porneia)*. Some view it strictly as "fornication" or "adultery." Others take it to mean "incest." A third group take it entirely out of the sexual realm and understand it as a "spiritual unfaithfulness," similar to that of Gomer, the wife of Hosea. This is another case where the meaning must fall somewhere between a strict understanding and one which is completely open-ended. The best solution is to see it as any illicit hetero- or homosexual activity which violates the sacred trust of the one-flesh principle.[7]

It should be added quickly that although divorce is allowed by this exception, in no sense is it compulsory. Quite the contrary. The thrust of the indissolubility of marriage and the gospel spirit of forgiveness plead for reconciliation. I have seen a number of relationships that have been renewed and strengthened after a violation by one or both of the spouses. It is hard work and demands a great deal of frank discussion and a willingness to forgive. But once this sort of surgery has been performed, healing and renewed strength can develop. However, in cases where the roguery has so shattered the foundation of the marriage, or where repentance is not forthcoming, divorce is permitted.

Paul on Divorce: 1 Corinthians 7:10-16
Paul's first letter to the church at Corinth is an epistle for

confused and immature Christians. Their pagan background and environment make it difficult for them to discern Christian truth and apply it. Paul, in addressing the problem of divorce, begins by referring to the words of Jesus regarding the indissolubility of marriage (1 Cor 7: 10-11). Christian spouses should stay together and not voluntarily separate from one another. I assume that the Corinthians, like the audiences of Luke and Mark, knew the exception clause of Jesus. After all, it was contained in the Sermon on the Mount, and this sermon was one of the earliest set of teachings to be orally transmitted throughout the Christian churches.

If, however, a Christian spouse should be disobedient to this word, then that person should either remain unmarried or be reconciled to his or her spouse. Again, as with the Mosaic legislation, this is not intended to encourage the practice, but simply to regulate abnormal behavior.

Paul then takes up the case of a Christian married to a nonbeliever (vv. 12-16). If the nonbeliever consents to stay, then the Christian is to make no overture toward separation. In fact, if the believing spouse follows the guidelines of 1 Peter 3:1-7, a mixed marriage may have missionary potential. As the unbeliever is exposed to the genuine faith of the believer, the Holy Spirit begins to woo the mate into God's family. The Spirit's work may certainly be rejected, but it cannot be denied that it is there in an extraordinary measure. If the unbeliever rejects the call of God and chooses to leave his spouse, either by mutual agreement or desertion, then the believing partner is no longer under obligation to keep the marriage together. Paul himself may have suffered this trauma.

Follow the Directions
Dwight Small says, "People would not get divorced for such trivial reasons if they did not get married for such trivial

reasons."[8] Marriage cannot be viewed as a "trial-run, 30-day-money-back-guarantee-if-you-are-not-completely-satisfied" product. Rather, it is a lifelong covenant which is witnessed by God and only dissolved by a sinful, disobedient act of at least one of the spouses. More often than not it is a reciprocal action by both. Today there is a rash of evangelical books on how it *feels* to be divorced. Many of these books espouse a secular philosophy of life. They echo the feeling of a book jacket I saw in a used-book store, *Divorce: The Way Things Are, Not The Way Things Should Be.*

Again, stereotypes and generalizations must be banished in order to see each situation with the empathy and thoughtfulness it deserves. But we cannot retreat from maintaining that the dissolving of the marriage covenant, unless specific permission is given in Scripture, is contrary to God's revealed will. It is sin and should be dealt with appropriately. One writer tells us that he "set out a fleece" to know if God would let him out of his marriage. Surely this type of guidance can do nothing but bring us into absolute confusion in every area. There is in some quarters a cry for open-mindedness. But being open-minded can often mean having a mind too porous to hold any conviction. God's Word—not our fleece, not our reason, not our emotions—is our plumb line. In empathy, we may want to create new exceptions for divorce and remarriage, but this can only bring us additional heartache and perplexity.

To make sure all this information fits together in some orderly fashion, let's restate some of our conclusions:

1. Divorce is permitted, though not compulsory, in cases where illicit hetero- or homosexual activity has violated the sacred trust of the one-flesh principle.

2. Though divorce is permitted, the spirit of forgiveness in the gospel begs for reconciliation even when there is a violation of the one-flesh trust. No one should underestimate the difficulty of such reconciliation nor undervalue

its potential benefits. Some Christians, in an effort to quickly patch up the relationship, are often insensitive to the real cost of forgiveness. Forgiveness involves sacrifice. There must be a sacrifice of pride, of the vision once held of the other person, and of resentment. There must be a willingness to withstand the disapproval of friends and relatives. But like the father of the prodigal son, we must be prepared to forgive and rejoice when there is true repentance (Lk 15:22-24).

3. Divorce for any other cause than sexual immorality and subsequent remarriage is viewed as adultery since the first marriage has never been legitimately dissolved.

4. Scripture allows for the possibility of two Christians separating from bed and board, although not divorcing one another. In such a case, they are to remain in a celibate state or to rejoin one another.

5. Desertion, initiated by an unbelieving partner, is sufficient cause for dissolving a marriage. In such a case, there is nothing wrong with the deserted believer beginning the necessary legal work for the termination of the marriage.

6. In a mixed marriage where there is physical abuse or emotional desertion of the believing partner, the church may want to encourage a temporary separation of bed and board. This is not intended to be the first step toward divorce, for neither of these grounds biblically justify divorce. However, concern for the emotional and physical safety of the spouse and any children demands that some action be taken. As I will suggest later on, this period of separation can be a time in which the church aids the family in reconstructing the marriage.

7. In cases where permanent desertion is initiated by a professing Christian, such a person should be excommunicated until such time that repentance and reconciliation takes place.

8. Where the Bible permits divorce it also allows remar-

riage. I do not believe that the words of Jesus lend the interpretation that innocent parties or deserted spouses cannot remarry. Guy Duty's *Divorce and Remarriage* argues this point most persuasively.

9. The church constantly keeps the doorway of repentance and reconciliation open to every disobedient Christian. Divorce, even when contrary to Scripture, is not the unforgivable sin. Forgiveness and reinstatement to the believing community and to marriage is possible. As the official statement of the United Presbyterian Church in the U.S.A. says, "Restitution is possible when a sufficient penitence for sin and failure is evident, and a firm purpose of an endeavor after Christian marriage is manifest."[9]

The church has often displayed a harsh attitude toward marital failure. "He made his bed, now let him lie in it!" But who among us have not made mistakes in our past for which we pleaded for a new start? Isn't it true that life is only understood when looking backwards, but must be lived looking forward? Then a new start is not out of the question. Under the supervision of the pastoring community forgiveness can be mediated, reconstructed marital patterns can be fostered, and the intention for permanency in marriage can be secured. For the divorced Christian there can be "the oil of gladness instead of mourning, the mantle of praise instead of a faint spirit" (Is 61:3).

Separation and Reconciliation
Christians are not immune from marital failure. Some couples are so bound by destructive habit patterns that their only hope for relief seems to be divorce. But the church must offer a different hope for the ailing marriage. Specifically, couples experiencing difficulty need to learn new patterns of behavior. Sometimes the relationship may already involve so much stress that the church will find it necessary to suggest separation. But this separation should not just be

a separation from one another, but a separation to something else.

The couple should submit their marriage to the protective custody of the church. The conflict then comes under the authority of the Christian community. Serving in a parental role the community seeks to lead the couple in a renegotiation of the marital contract. This obviously cannot be done in a one-hour-per-week counseling program. What is needed is that the separated couple live with Christian families and allow those families to function as surrogate parents. Courtship and dating can begin all over again. Ground rules can be established by both parties in order to see that a healthy relationship develops.

The separation should last for a designated amount of time. This insures that any instant make-up will not fall apart within a few days. Sexual ground rules must be discussed and delineated. Specific time should be arranged for the couple to be alone and to talk, as well as time to talk together with their parental overseers. Churches which have taken this responsibility seriously, rather than just letting the couple float into the world of single bars and lonely apartments, are succeeding in seeing the restoration of entire families. In saying this, in no way am I forgetting the responsibility of the couple. They must be willing to work at rescuing their marriage, even if there is no tangible evidence for survival at the beginning. With their cooperation and the sensitive counsel of the church, broken marriages can be restored.

Only after every effort of reconciliation has been made does the church have the freedom to allow the separation to be permanent. However, even then it is expected that no remarriage will take place. The marriage is viewed as intact, though there has been a separation of bed and board. Any infidelity in this separated state constitutes grounds for divorce and the discipline of the person.

Therefore when the church permits separation, it must spell out the entire ramifications of the action.

Cast Out the Seed of Divorce

There are several implications of what I have said thus far. The first is that Christians ought to reject wholesale any thought of divorce. Believers are not to entertain the idea; for them it is not an option. "Well," you might respond, "what about the exceptions?" That's what they are—exceptions and not the rule. So when you are attracted to the fifty-dollar divorce packet, or hear the outlandish hyperbole "liberated divorcée," or begin to sing "Fifty Ways to Leave Your Lover," cast that seed out of your mind. Jesus made clear that the wandering mind is fertile soil for divorce (Mt 5:27-32). Our minds must be disciplined for the building up of marriage. This cannot happen if we are harboring in the crevice of our minds the secular option of divorce. This warning is especially needed by those who have divorce patterns in their immediate family. For it seems that the domino theory applies in divorce: when one falls, they all can fall.

Once divorce occurs, it's too late to discuss marriage. The horse is already out of the barn. Therefore, the Christian church must continually talk about marriage. We must read about it. We must pray for it. We must honor it. We must exhort one another in it. Single people need to tolerate us at this point (I should point out that we also need to constantly review God's calling for the unmarried, widowed and divorced), but marriage needs to be built up and protected.

To insure a healthy marriage, every church should provide at least four premarital and two postmarital counseling sessions with each new couple.[10] Stress should be placed upon the relational irritants and communication barriers that are present in every marriage. Couples need to learn how to argue, how to forgive, how to forget, how to love. Each couple needs to know that all marriages have problems and that they are not insurmountable. They should be encouraged not to live their marriage as though it were a self-supporting terrarium plant, but to call unashamedly on the body of Christ when help is needed.

Every couple should also be members of a household fellowship group. If you have ever attended a rock concert, you will remember that each of the singers has a speaker facing him in order to hear the harmonies being sung by the other members of the group. In the same way, a household fellowship group which focuses on Bible study, transparent sharing and prayer provides a feedback system for its members. It is able to pick up and feed back the harmony as well as the dissonance that is given off in the marriages represented.

While driving in downtown Vancouver one day, I heard the radio DJ report that the weather in the city was just beautiful. There was one problem, however; he was in an underground news studio reading the weather report and I was above ground—and the weather was miserable! Often Christians in marriage are like this. They want to give a glowing report of a beautiful marriage, but it does not match what they are actually experiencing. As married Christians we need not be intimidated by the thought that our marital relationship needs enrichment from time to time. We must admit when not all is well. Marriage takes work, and there is more to be learned and put into practice than most of us have discovered.

A Healing Community

The church, as revealed in the New Testament, is to be a relational, charismatically endowed community. As a community it is called to model the life of Jesus in reconciliation and servanthood. Its mandate is to heal the brokenhearted and to give hope in the midst of despair. It is not shocked by sinners, for that is whom Jesus came to save. Neither is it shocked to discover a sinner in its own midst. The church knows that we are all in the process of transformation "from one degree of glory to another." When a marriage hits turbulent winds, it needs the anchor of a second-mile community to ride out the storm. Midnight conversations, free baby-sitting and a spare bedroom should be only a phone call away. At these times an ounce of demonstration is worth more than a ton of speculation. And who will be shocked or unduly upset that such marital conflicts erupt in the Christian community? Only those whose pride forbids them from seeing that except for the grace of God they too could be in this predicament.

The story is told of a team of Alpine climbers who, during the course of their descent, lost several of their companions in an accident. When queried by the authorities as to what they did to prevent the accident, each of the survivors displayed his rope-burned hands. We may not be able to save every marital failure, but at least we should display the rope burns of a community who did everything in its power to save the marriage.

Take Heed to Your Spirit
While studying the problem of divorce, I read a brilliant development of the exception clause in Matthew and its relationship to Mark and Luke. It was an insightful piece of reasoning and exegesis. The only fly in the ointment was that the author of the commentary had divorced his wife and remarried another woman without any apparent biblical warrant. This did not make his exegesis invalid, but it did reveal that it takes more than a proper doctrine of marriage to keep our marriages intact. As Malachi warned, it is our spirits that need to be guarded as we begin to plot avenues of solving our monotony with monogamy (Mal

2:15 NASB). We must pray, "Lord, I need your Spirit working in my life. I could rationalize myself out of this marriage. I know that the consideration of divorce is only a manifestation of the bankrupt state of my spirit. Take me. Mold me. With the eyes of faith, I believe you can bring about a marvelous transformation of this marriage. Show me the people in the Christian community who can help me in this restoration. I'm yours. I will not go in any direction unless you lead."

In 1977 a crowded country club in the eastern part of the United States burned down, killing a number of people. Just after the fire broke out a young busboy ran through the club announcing the danger. But only a few heeded his word and escaped. The rest waited till too late and were trapped. I believe the Spirit of God desires the church to serve as this busboy to the world—to warn of the impending danger, to affirm the benefits of the functioning family unit, and to make known the consequences of its erosion. Yet beyond this the Spirit has a word for the church itself. Isn't it time that we got our own house in order? Is the credibility of our own family life sufficient to proclaim such a warning? Have we tolerated an unbiblical standard of divorce? Have we offered a new start to those who have failed and are now suffering? "For the time has come for judgment to begin with the household of God; and if it begins with us, what will be the end of those who do not obey the gospel of God?" (1 Pet 4:17).

Tithe If You
Love Jesus—
Anyone Can
Honk

8

Gary was a third-year dental student when I first met him.
As a committed Christian, he had foregone a salaried summer job to work in a project of evangelism and discipleship.
Three months before that project began Gary went into a
convulsive seizure because of a brain tumor. Corrective
surgery saw him well and on his feet six weeks later. In
June, Gary moved into a large southern-style house, along
with my wife and me and twenty-four other students. The
first flush of communal love had just about run its course
when one of our members encountered a bill collector at
the door. Unbeknown to Gary, he still owed five hundred
dollars for his surgery.

Gary had no money. My wife and I were living on four
hundred dollars a month and attempting to save for grad-
uate school. And the other students, well, they had spent all
their money in the previous spring term. At first the
thought of paying off the debt seemed impossible. At the
same time we realized that God was calling us to give active
expression to the fact that we were one body. My brother's
financial debt was my financial debt. That evening we

passed a discarded cigar box and asked everyone to donate what they could. Watching the expression of each student, I could tell that it was a challenge to their faith. Would they place their brother's financial need before their own? Would they adopt what C. S. Lewis called the Christian grammar, "first person he, second person you and third person I"? Impatiently we tallied the results. Over one thousand dollars had been placed in the box. Some had relinquished the entire contents of their checking and saving accounts, giving their last penny.

We quickly paid off Gary's bill and decided to share in common the remaining five hundred dollars. Whenever there was a need for shaving cream or gasoline, each person took what was needed. I kept close watch on the contents wondering when the surplus would be consumed. But like the widow's provision, "the jar of meal was not spent, neither did the cruse of oil fail" (1 Kings 17:16). For the remaining two months all our material needs were provided. Soon people found out about our sharing in Gary's need and the continuing lifestyle of having all things in common. Several businessmen openly wept when they saw this demonstration of sacrificial love. Later, as though it were a resurrection of New Testament history, dozens were added to the body of Christ because of this powerful testimony.

This one event, along with several others like it, convinced me that God would glorify himself through our financial stewardship. People would be attracted to the gospel if they observed a sacrificial demonstration of our love for one another. Sadly, such testimony is lacking in much of the church. The church is so encumbered with mortgage payments and the financial maintenance of its institutions, it cannot respond to the genuine needs of God's worldwide community. Personal affluency among North American evangelicals is at an all-time high, but millions of other Christians suffer from malnutrition, lack of adequate shelter, polluted water and inadequate health care. These members of Christ's body, connected to us through the Spirit, suffer, yet we make no effort to re-arrange our financial priorities. The covetous, stingy, wasteful and consumptive use of our financial resources is the blight of the American evangelical church of the twenti-eth century.

Several years ago I saw a play about the Chinese revolu-tion called *Fanshen. Fanshen* means to "turn about, to make a revolution." The three-act drama reveals the unsophisti-cated thinking of revolutionaries that believe only one *fan-shen* is necessary—one violent overthrow of the wealthy landlords and corrupt government officials. But as time goes on, it becomes obvious to everyone that it is necessary that there be several *fanshens,* constant revolution.

The Christian church has a similar word in its vocabu-lary: *Repentance* means "to turn about." It is not just to be sorry, but to let one's sorrow issue in changed behavior. The church must be in constant revolution from its sinful disobedience. We must continually bring forth "fruit that befits our repentance" (Mt 3:8). Conversion repentance is the first step in a lifetime of repentant behavior, and re-pentance in our stewardship sins is one area where the church needs to give its attention today. Therefore, Mala-chi's word to fifth-century B.C. Israel is just as relevant today as it ever was.

Bringing the Whole Tithe into the Storehouse

Have you seen the bumper sticker which says, "Tithe if you love Jesus—anyone can honk"? Not a bad idea, but I won-der how many Christians know the basic tithing require-ments of the Old Testament. Tithing is God's catechism for sacrificial giving, and it is therefore helpful for every Chris-tian to understand.

131

Abraham, after defeating Chedorlaomer, the king of Elam, and his confederates, gave a tenth of all his goods to Melchizedek, the priest of God Most High (Gen 14:1-24; Heb 7:1-3). Abraham's tithe did not come from the spoils which he had taken, for he refused to take booty. Rather his tithe came from his own reserves. This was an act of sacrificial worship, acknowledging the blessing of God in the defeat of his enemies. Two generations later, Jacob experienced a vivid dream detailing God's future blessing on him and his descendants. When he awoke, Jacob covenanted to give God ten per cent of all that was to be his (Gen 28:18-22).

Under Mosaic law every Israelite family was required to give ten per cent of their seed, fruit and herd each year (Lev 27:30-33; Deut 14:22). These offerings were not given all at once, but prorated over the course of the year. Portions were to be given at each of the three major festivals: passover, weeks (also called Pentecost), and booths (Deut 16). Israel was not to appear before the Lord empty-handed but to come with the bounty with which they had been blessed. After giving a basket of first fruits to the Levitical priest, who placed it before the altar, the worshiper was to pray the following prayer:

And you shall make response before the LORD your God, "A wandering Aramean was my father; and he went down into Egypt and sojourned there, few in number; and there he became a nation, great, mighty, and populous. And the Egyptians treated us harshly, and afflicted us, and laid upon us hard bondage. Then we cried to the LORD the God of our fathers, and the LORD heard our voice and saw our affliction, our toil, and our oppression; and the LORD brought us out of Egypt with a mighty hand and an outstretched arm, with great terror, with signs and wonders; and he brought us into this place and gave us this land, a land flowing with milk and honey.

And behold, now I bring the first of the fruit of the ground, which thou, O LORD, hast given me." And you shall set it down before the LORD your God, and worship before the LORD your God. (Deut 26:5-10)

Every third year offered a variation in the tithing scheme. On these years the tithe was collected in one's home town rather than being offered in Jerusalem (Deut 14:28-29; 26:12-15). The focus of this contribution was to aid the poor and needy of the city as well as to finance the priestly class.

Freewill offerings, as the term suggests, were voluntary gifts, acknowledging God's abundant kindness (Deut 16:10). These special sacrifices and offerings could be given for a variety of reasons: a vow taken (Lev 27), cleansing from leprosy (Lev 14), purification after childbirth (Lev 12), consecration of a priest (Lev 8—9), release from a Nazarite vow (Num 6), days of national repentance (Judg 20:26; 1 Sam 7) or preparation for battle (1 Sam 13:8-9; Ps 20).

In case you are keeping count of the total obligation inherent in the Old Testament legislation, you must also add travel expenses. Israel's worship was centralized worship. Sacrifices were accepted only in selected places. With the arrival of the monarchy under Saul and later David, the place of centralized worship was in Jerusalem. So each family was to go to Jerusalem to sacrifice. If the distance was too far to carry grain or drive herds, it was permissible to sell your goods and to buy others when you arrived in Jerusalem. Travel time was often two or three days of walking and often involved expense for lodging and refreshment.

Tithing in Israel thus did not mean a mere ten per cent. As you can see, the actual percentage of one's yearly income given in tithe or offerings could run anywhere from fifteen to thirty per cent. It is much more accurate to say that

Israel gave one-fifth to one-third rather than one-tenth of its resources back to God. Some would counter by saying that Israel gave this much because they had no state or federal taxes to pay. That is not so. God, through Samuel the prophet, warned that the by-product of a desire for a king would be taxation and conscription (1 Sam 8:10-18). Revenue was necessary to run the monarchy and the accompanying necessities. And even if Israel's own kings were not collecting taxes, you can bet that the foreign invaders from the eighth century B.C. on certainly did. So there was taxation as well as tithing and sacrificial giving.

God Owns Me
The motivation for tithing was never to placate God or to attempt to win his favor. Rather, in obedience to God's revelation, tithing was a testimony to God's ownership— a sign that he owned you. God is the owner of all things. We are simply managers of God's property. Tithing is giving back to God that which is already his in the first place. Scripture is clear that God wants us before our tithes, but it also emphasizes that God has all of you when he has all of your tithe.

I will never forget filing my first income tax form after graduating from the university. I had spent that year in student ministry. Though the remuneration was minimal, I wanted some outside counsel in filing my income tax, so I went to a low-cost tax specialist. As I waited my turn in the office I felt strangely out of place. It was obvious by the clothing worn and cars parked in front of the office that I was out of my league. I barely made enough to even pay any tax.

When the tax specialist looked at my income and at the amount given to charitable donations, he leaned back in his chair and eyed me with the question, "Who owns you, boy?" He went on to express amazement that my wife and I would so freely share with others. His day had been full of people who had everything they needed, but shared nothing with anyone. He went on to explain that less than one per cent of his clients ever itemized charitable deductions; they simply accepted the basic deduction given to them by the government. Tithing is a testimony of God's ownership. It will not always be as public as this, but it should always be evident that we are not our own—we have been bought with a price (1 Cor 6:19-20).

Quite naturally, the question arises whether or not the New Testament teaches tithing. Ostensibly, stewardship legislation is like many other Old Testament laws, when given their messianic interpretation they are not abolished, but amplified (Mt 5:17-48). Not only does the basic stipulation prevail, but a greater principle is revealed. The recollections of the Apostolic Fathers, the leaders of the second-century church, confirm that the early church practiced tithing, but it also practiced a greater principle. Before we speak of that principle, let us take a look at ourselves for a moment.

Lessons from an Old Card Shark
Permit me to admit a vice I nurtured in my university days. I was a card player from the word go. Spades, hearts—I loved any game that didn't take money. Over one Christmas holiday I began to teach my children the fine art of card playing. Since they were only three and five years old, I had to start at an elementary level. So we began with Old Maid.

First I taught the children to shuffle, then to deal and finally to arrange their cards in the proper order. Next, they had to learn to keep a straight face and not let their opponents see their cards. It did not take the five-year-old long to realize that a quick and observant eye could detect the holdings of the three-year-old. So I kept repeating to the children, "You must keep your cards very close to you so that no one will see what you have!" A few weeks later I began to preach on the subject of economic lifestyles. During my preparation, one of our community members phoned me. "George," he said, "you need to be very careful in dealing with financial lifestyles. A lot of Christians are very fearful; they keep their financial cards very close to them." The Christian church has been telling its members exactly what I told Eryn Faye and Scott, "Keep a poker face, and keep your cards close to you."

The overwhelming need for Christians to share their financial resources is clearly visible. There is evidence that many are responding to these needs. However, at the same time we hide those cards that reveal how much we spend on life insurance, on going out to dinner, on holidays and recreational equipment, on clothing and our favorite hobby. Last, unless we happen to be the pastor whose salary is published in the church budget, how many people know how much we earn? We hide behind a curtain of economic privacy. The church may have its ten per cent—though statistics show this is seldom so—but the rest is mine. And you can keep your nose out of it, thank you. This is a non-negotiable item. We don't even want to talk about it.

Studying economic lifestyles taught our community a great deal. But there was a lot of plowing to be done before God could plant the seed of his Word in our hearts. We asked people in their home study groups what they wanted to teach them about an alternate economic lifestyle. Transparency, by some, caused us all to admit that we did not want God to teach us anything new. In fact, we were very comfortable and did not want to be disturbed. Paradoxically, we knew at the same time that we did want God to work in our lives. We knew that we would not be free in Christ until our love affair with money was terminated. The process of scaling down our lifestyles and corralling our loose expenditures left us fearful and reluctant. But that was the area that God wanted to refine and cleanse. God wanted to glorify himself, and he was going to use our proper financial stewardship to do just that.

Four perspectives came into focus during this process, perspectives that I would encourage each church in North America to integrate into its community life. First, there are real needs in the world, and though we cannot meet them all, we can meet some. Second, we must begin to lay down our economic cards honestly with one another in order to rid ourselves of covetousness. Third, as our finances move more under Christ's control we will not be overwhelmed by guilt for what we have in comparison with others. We can believe that God has granted us these provisions and they are to be received thankfully (Phil 4:10-13). Last is a word from 1 John 5:3: "For this is the love of God, that we keep his commandments. And his commandments are not burdensome." Following Christ's commands will prove to be our liberation, not our captivity. Being yoked with Christ is both satisfying and rewarding.

For Your Sakes He Became Poor
The focal point of New Testament stewardship is in 2 Corinthians 8—9. Here we find that financial charity is no longer measured by percentage but by the activity of God's Son, who, though rich in his position with the Father, condescended to become man and die on a cross, in order that creation might be redeemed. Let me set the context for this model of sacrificial stewardship.

Paul, working in Macedonia among the churches of Philippi, Berea and Thessalonica, is writing to the Corinthians who are some two hundred miles south of him in the province of Achaia. He wants them to respond to the needs of the Jerusalem saints who are over a thousand miles away. Why is Jerusalem in need? Some people have suggested that it was due to the failure of the economic communalism that was practiced in Acts 2 and 4. That is almost impossible to substantiate. As Ronald Sider points out in *Rich Christians in an Age of Hunger,* the imperfect tense verbs ("they began selling," 2:45) suggests that the Christians did not sell all of their goods at one time, hence having nothing to fall back on in time of need, but that they were selling their goods and distributing the resources whenever there was need. He also suggests that there is a better explanation for the shortage.

First, Jerusalem was a city full of poor people. It was considered righteous to give alms in the Holy City, therefore a large number of beggars gathered there. In addition, there were the old who had come to Jerusalem to die and who existed exclusively on the handouts of the daily welfare basket. Jerusalem also had a large number of rabbis along with their disciples who lived off the charity of pilgrims to the city. Many of those converted in the early days of the church came from the lower socio-economic classes. Thus there was a need for immediate economic sharing among the believers (Acts 2:44-45).

Second, between A.D. 41 and 54 a number of natural disasters befell Jerusalem. Famine, earthquake and pestilence were not uncommon. During these difficult times rising prices were an everyday reality. Josephus records that in a matter of weeks four liters of wheat, the basic food staple, rose thirteen times its original price. And we gripe about double-digit inflation!

Third, as often was the case, Christians were discriminated against in employment practices because of their departure from Judaism. The Jerusalem saints were in an economic pinch, not of their own making, and needed the benevolent intervention of the Christian family. Christians at Antioch had already given to the Jerusalem saints. The same was true of the Macedonian Christians. Now Paul wants the Corinthians, who have already promised a gift, to complete their promise.[1]

The Push for the Buck

The story is told of a minister in a small town in the early days of the Canadian railroad. Every day, no matter what he was doing, he would rush out of his office to watch the daily express pass by. After a while, the members of his congregation began to view this eccentric behavior as slightly juvenile, so they asked him to give it up. He immediately refused. "No thank you, gentlemen," he asked, "I will preach your sermons, teach your Sunday-school classes, marry your young, bury your dead and run your charities. But I will not give up seeing that train go by. It's the only thing in this town that I don't have to push!"

I am sure this pastor would have loved the congregation in Macedonia. For Paul did not have to push these Christians to take seriously their economic responsibility for the Jerusalem saints (2 Cor 8:1-5). In fact, it appears that when Paul saw their own economic situation he was hesitant to even mention the need. Yet they bring the matter up and beg for the opportunity to minister in this financial way. Paul did not command them to give as might a cult leader. Neither did he command the Corinthians or beg them to give. He did not send out a computer-designed, graphically appealing "prayer" letter. Nor did he describe in vivid detail the plight of starving children in Jerusalem.

Lest you think that I am knocking any one group in particular, let me say that I think fund-raising is becoming a universal problem. Inflation is causing the stewardship pie to be cut into thinner and thinner pieces. Local churches are experiencing this reduction as well as parachurch movements. With this tightening of the money supply, parachurch organizations are making their needs known more and more vocally. Through every conceivable technique, organizations are making their appeals. Television is now being praised as the new Roman highway in gospel communication. Because of all this, the Year of the Evangelical has become the Year of the Media Appeal, and there is little doubt that much of this appeal has been tarnished by secularism. The question of extent is still out.

Christians need to hear the prophetic voice of an old television hack like Malcolm Muggeridge. He suggests that if Jesus were alive today his fourth temptation might be to take his gospel message on prime-time network television.[2] Though this may be extreme, there is no doubt that public fund raising has put evangelicals in an extremely vulnerable place.

Not only have appeals become secularized, so have our responses. Today, we wait for appeal letters or telethons before we respond. Whatever happened to Holy-Spirit-inspired listening and giving—the type of giving that fed the needs of George Müller and Hudson Taylor? These men had no media gimmicks to pull in the percentage funds. They simply prayed and believed God would move the hearts of Christians to respond to their needs.

Another question we must ask is, When will the church begin to live sacrificially for the sake of the kingdom? Many great missionary movements were launched by people who sold their possessions and gave the proceeds in order that the work might go forth. This is the sacrifice that is needed: People who will turn their tax rebates back into the work of the kingdom. People who will give up their excessive use of jewelry and plow that into the kingdom. People who will move into smaller homes and use the proceeds for the kingdom. People who will fast weekly and give the savings to the hungry of this world. The church must be alert to the ethics of fund raising and to the sacrificial passion that is necessary for the gospel to be spread throughout the world.[3]

Last, in this day of continuous financial appeals, stewardship should be in and through the local church. Some churches teach the principle of exclusive "storehouse tithing." This means that all the tithe is to be channeled in and through the local church. As a binding principle I do not find it valid. However, it is one way to resist the inundation of computer-appeal letters and guilt-laden media blitzes. As a body, the church gathers to pray through its stewardship. Goals are established that demand sacrifice on the part of everyone—goals broad enough to incorporate all types of ministries. Then together the community seeks prayerfully to meet those goals.

God's Grace to the Macedonians

If Paul was not badgering them, how was it that the Macedonians gave so freely? We don't need to be overly pious and suppose that Paul never said a word about the situation in Jerusalem. Surely, he gave them some information, though it appears not to be much. This avalanche of generosity was launched by the grace of God. It was Holy-Spirit-inspired freedom from possessions and an emancipation to give. It was God's movement that produced this spirit of charity.

Anne Watson, the wife of the Reverend David Watson of York, England, shared with us her experience in community living. Anne suggested that if we could not invite our neighbors into our homes, take them to our closets and freely give them everything in our wardrobes, then we were being possessed by our possessions. With that illustration in mind, consider what grace must fall on you to produce this type of liberality. That is the kind of grace that fell on the Macedonians.

Paul wants the same thing to happen to the Corinthians. He reminds them that they have all the spiritual gifts (2 Cor 8:7). In a section that reminds us of 1 Corinthians 12—14, he wants to know if they have love. By comparison of their earnestness with that of the Macedonians, he wants to prove the sincerity of the Corinthian love. The Greek word for *genuineness (gnēsios)* is used of a legitimate child as opposed to one who is illegitimate. Paul questions the Corinthians, "Are you legitimate offspring of the God of love? Have you been baptized by the Spirit of love and graciousness? If you have, then complete your intention of meeting this need."

For the Apostle Paul, as well as the other apostles, response to the divine yes entails a host of additional yeses. When I see my brother or sister in need, I will not slam the door of my heart and cover my head with my Scandinavian blanket, but I will arise and meet that need, even if it means giving my own blanket. To follow Jesus Christ is a commitment to the fraternity of those who go the second mile for their neighbor.

The amazing thing about the Macedonian churches was not how much they gave, but their economic state when they gave. They were suffering from what William Barclay calls "rock bottom poverty." It was abject poverty which demanded dependence on others for daily bread—the type of poverty which in spiritual terms is commended by Jesus in the Sermon on the Mount (Mt 5:3). The reason for their deprivation is unknown. It is possible that they were suffering from job discrimination similar to the Jerusalem saints. In spite of their hardship, they stood together and gave beyond expectation. How overwhelming when you consider that the average North American churchman gives less than two hundred dollars a year to his local church! It may be popular to speak of the Year of the Evangelical and of fifty million born-again Christians, but statistics reveal that our pocketbooks are still unbaptized.

Paul goes on to argue that it is not the amount that is important, echoing Jesus' commendation of the widow's mite, but the readiness to sacrifice. What we give is to be proportional to what we have, not to what we don't have (2 Cor 8:12). Students still waiting to pull down their first salaries are nevertheless called upon to give now. People waiting for raises in salary or for inflation to abate are still called upon to give proportionally to what they earn now.

Don't Look Now, Here Comes the Offering Plate

I wonder what goes through your mind each Sunday as the offering plate passes by. Do you think of it as just another ritual of the church? A necessary evil which the church should banish? In the early years of our community, we did not pass an offering plate but attached a collection box to the wall in the vestibule. For its attempts at privacy and dethroning the high profile of finances in a church it should be applauded. But it dawned on me one day that this treatment of our finances was really saying that money is ignoble and has no place in the worship of the church. Why shouldn't we collect our tithes and offerings in the worship hour? Isn't this the practical completion, a concrete manifestation of our worship? Though the offering should not be elevated to the place of a sacrament, neither should it be shoved into an irreverent corner or treated as a comma in the grammar of the liturgy.

Notice the attitude of the Macedonians regarding their stewardship (2 Cor 8:4). Paul uses three great Christian words to describe their financial contribution. They were continually begging Paul for the *favor* (*charis,* "the grace or gift") of *participation* (*koinōnia,* "fellowship") in the *support* (*diakonia,* "service or ministry") of the saints. They were begging for the gift to be able to give. We usually associate gifts with receiving, but they wanted the privilege of giving. Their participation with the Jerusalem saints was to be a fellowship. We think of fellowship as cookies and punch around the piano, but New Testament fellowship is rooted in the idea of economic sharing, of financial participation which works in relieving the pain and hunger of suffering brothers and sisters.

Last, the Macedonians saw their giving as service or ministry. Stewardship is as much a ministry to the body as evangelism, preaching or folding chairs. It is serving others through our financial resources. Harry Emerson Fosdick, the famous New York preacher from Riverside Church, once said: "A dollar is a miraculous thing. It is a man's personal energy reduced to portable form and endowed with powers that the man himself does not possess. It can go where he cannot go; speak languages he cannot speak; lift burdens he cannot touch with his fingers; save lives with which he cannot directly deal—so that a man busy all day downtown can at the same time be working in a boys' club, hospital, settlement and children's centers all over the world."

It appears from the hesitation of the Corinthians that Paul was being criticized by some of the leaders of this Achaian church. Perhaps they accused him of imposing hardship on the Corinthians in order to put the Jerusalem saints at ease (2 Cor 8:13-14). The heart of Paul's response is one of the best kept secrets in the evangelical church today. In fact, most evangelicals have responded to this statement like the wife of the Bishop of Woolwich who greeted the news of Darwin's discoveries with, "Let's hope that it isn't true and, if it is, that it won't become generally known." Paul replies, "For this is not for the ease of others and for your affliction, but by way of equality" (2 Cor 8:13 NASB). His argument supposes that none shall be afflicted and that none should be at ease, but that each shall have equally. Every Christian has what he needs and no one is lacking. Geographic separation does not demand or allow economic inequality. It does not matter that Jerusalem is over one thousand miles away, for equality knows no geographical boundary among Christians.

I'm afraid that many of us today are practicing the idea of "all of us are equal, but some of us are more equal than others," rather than the equality of Scripture. But we are not owners, we are stewards. We take what we need and share the rest. Hoarding only brings mildew (Ex 16:16-21) and death.

The exhortation of Malachi concerning tithing contains with it a promise of blessing. "Bring the full tithes into the storehouse, that there may be food in my house; and thereby put me to the test, says the LORD of hosts, if I will not open the windows of heaven for you and pour down for you an overflowing blessing" (Mal 3:10). This is a promise which evangelicals will not want to overlook given the foreboding expectations of the 1980s. The church has all the money it needs. What is needed now is a Holy-Spirit-inspired release of that money in order that God's priorities can be furthered. His priorities are that none of the 700 million Christians in the world should be without, and that none should be hoarding for his own use.

We
Gotta
Have
More

9

Two hundred gay-rights activists had gathered to protest a rally in our city being conducted by a Christian television personality known for his anti-gay sentiments. There were a few disruptions as people entered the building, but by and large the meeting was peaceful. Then a television camera caught a wide-angle pan of some Christians walking through the picket line holding their noses. That picture did more damage than a thousand words.

Scripture is clear that those who practice a lifestyle of homosexuality "will not inherit the kingdom of God" (1 Cor 6:9-10). Neither will the person who abides in a lifestyle of adultery or fornication. However, periodically Christians single out a group of sinners and pronounce their sins to be the most injurious. We seem to forget that the call to moral rearmament is impossible for the man or woman bound in the spell of Satan's lie (Eph 2:1-10). Only the grace of God can retrieve wrecked and perverted lives. We need to remind ourselves of the advice that Paul gives to the Corinthians: God will judge the world for its sin. You judge the church. You judge your own house (1 Cor. 5:9-13).

In judging our own house, it is amazing how selective we can be. For the sin of covetousness is spoken of as harshly as the sin of homosexuality or adultery. We complain loudly of certain sins, but we ignore others completely. The Decalog is clear: "You shall not covet your neighbor's house; you shall not covet your neighbor's wife, or his manservant, or his maidservant, or his ox, or his ass, or anything that is your neighbor's" (Ex 20:17). Paul's advice is that the church should disassociate itself from any Christian who is living covetously (1 Cor 5:11). Covetousness is idolatry (Col 3:5). It is the worship of a false god. Such persons cannot possibly inherit the kingdom of God (1 Cor 6:9-10).

How many times have you seen a covetous person disciplined in the church? That's foreign to our experience, isn't it? By and large, covetousness is accepted as a way of life in the evangelical church. It's the American way. The covetous person is the enterprising business person. He's not covetous, he's bullish. Rather than being disciplined, this person is coddled and pampered and encouraged to earn more so that he can give to "God's work." This person may be the engineer of a blockbusting real estate agency, or a pyramid corporation, or a slickly worded insurance scheme, just as long as he is there on Sunday, tithe in hand. It's a necessary evil—something we love and need too much to abolish.

There is nothing in the Christian that makes him less vulnerable in this area than any other person. At present, North America is suffering an epidemic of covetousness. One half of all items in retail stores did not even exist ten years ago. But today, we are compelled to have the latest new gadget. Microwave ovens, pocket calculators, water picks and eyeglasses that match your wardrobe have become part of our lives. And what do we do with all these things? We store them in our rental shelters. Television commercials are designed, not just to inform, but to create desire.

The average American spends nine years of his life watching television; therefore the desire to possess more constantly increases. In Canada, with a population of twenty-three million, which is smaller than that of California, the personal indebtedness of its citizens is twenty-three billion dollars. That is one thousand dollars for every man, woman and child in the country. Statistics Canada reports that only a small percentage of that is mortgage money. Most of the indebtedness is owed to bank and retail credit cards. Our federal government, much like that of the U.S., is itself indebted to the tune of seventy billion dollars. For this, we pay about nine billion dollars yearly in interest. To evangelicals, living in a culture of greed, can we not hear the Lord speaking to us through the Apostle Paul? "Don't let the world around you squeeze you into its own mold, but let God remold your minds from within, so that you may prove in practice that the plan of God for you is good, meets all his demands and moves toward the goal of true maturity (Rom 12:2 Phillips).

A Last Minute Bout with Stinginess
To ensure that the Corinthians will be ready with their gift when the Apostle arrives, Paul sends Timothy and two assistants ahead to make preparation for the offering (2 Cor 8:16-24). "So I thought it necessary to urge the brethren that they would go on ahead to you and arrange beforehand your previously promised bountiful gift, that the same might be ready as a bountiful gift, and not affected by covetousness" (2 Cor 9:5 NASB). *Covetousness* (*pleonexia*) literally means "a desire to have more." Paul is worried that the Corinthians may suffer a last minute bout of stinginess, causing them to forsake a liberal offering. In fear, the Corinthians might cry out like Israel in Malachi's day, "I need more for myself!" Paul is aware though that covetousness comes from comparing ourselves with others.

When I see my neighbor's possessions, something ignites within me that desires to have what is his. Covetousness is an example of practical determinism. I am being determined by my neighbor's state rather than determining my own. But the gospel of Christ is meant to set us free from this kind of determinism. Through its power we have the ability to make proper biblical choices, independent of pressure from others. We have been set free from the compulsion to have more (Rom 6:6-7).

Paul goes on to answer the practical question, "If I give and give sacrificially, will there be enough left over for me?" "God," he says, "is able to provide you with every blessing in abundance, so that you may always have enough of everything and may provide in abundance for every good work" (2 Cor 9:8). There will be sufficiency for your need and abundance to share. If you are ready to give, then God will make it possible for you to give and meet your own needs at the same time. Let me emphasize though that this promised abundance is for liberality, not testimony. I have no sympathy with pep rallies for prosperity or testimonies of how Jesus made me rich. Far too many Christians want the security of riches rather than the stewardship of wealth. Like Linus we want to be the humble country doctor who drives a Rolls Royce.

It has been said that history would stop repeating itself if we would learn the lessons it has already taught. John Wesley two centuries ago warned, "I fear, wherever riches have increased, the essence of religion has decreased in the same proportion. Therefore, do I not see how it is possible, in the nature of things, for any revival of true religion to continue long. For religion must necessarily produce both industry and frugality; and these cannot but produce riches. But as riches increase, so will pride, and anger, and the love for the world and all of its branches."[1] Mary Cosby of the Church of the Saviour in Washington, D.C., calls this process the "monastic cycle." Devotion brings discipline, which produces abundance, which destroys both devotion and discipline.

One more idea along this line. Christians have assumed from their readings in the Old Testament that material prosperity is a sign of God's blessing. This principle can be established from a number of texts. However, it needs to be said just as explicitly that material prosperity may also be a sign of an unethical or immoral behavior (Jer 12:1-2).[2] Eighth-century Israel had a number of prosperous people when the prophet Amos paid them a visit. He announced to them that their riches had not come as a blessing for righteousness, but as a result of their neglect and harsh treatment of the poor. The rich were wealthy at the expense of the oppressed. Amos does not tell them to count their blessings, name them one by one, but to repent, unless the day of the Lord should come as judgment instead of reward (Amos 4:1; 5:10-13, 18-20; 6:1—9:15).

The example of Jesus is that of poverty and simplicity. The gospel is not an economic insurance policy which guarantees you all you ever wanted but could not afford.[3] Jesus calls us to repent of our covetousness, not to baptize it as a disguised servant of the church. Jesus is Lord, not Mammon. The words of prison reformer Sir Alexander Peterson need to be the watchword of the church today; "Lord, make us masters of ourselves that we may be the servants of others."[4]

Where Does All the Money Go?

If the New Testament presupposes the suspension of the Levitical priesthood and the cultus, what is to be the focus of our stewardship? A Christian's first responsibility is to his family. "If any one does not provide for his relatives, and especially for those of his own family, he has disowned the faith and is worse than an unbeliever" (1 Tim 5:8).

151

This responsibility entails provisions for shelter, clothing, health care and education. It also involves monitoring necessities as opposed to luxuries, needs versus greeds. Such action should not be a unilateral activity of the father or the parents. Because of the status pressure on our children, they need to be involved in the decision-making process. Not that they have the final say, but they need to know that their wants are being heard and that the principles governing financial decisions apply equally to everyone, including their parents. Children must see that their parents are not being stingy but are living under the liberating canopy of Christ's lordship.

Christian stewardship also involves the support of itinerant and residential workers, local and international. The advance of the kingdom will necessitate some workers who are freed from financial maintenance in order to dedicate themselves to the tasks of evangelism, discipleship, prayer and the meeting of physical needs. Jesus and his disciples were supported in such a manner, for the most part by a group of women (Lk 8:1-3). The Apostles in Acts 6 gave themselves exclusively to prayer and teaching. In turn, the church provided for their welfare. Paul insists in his epistles that those who work for the gospel have the right to earn their living by the gospel (Gal 6:6; 1 Tim 5:17-18). Though Paul never asserted this right for himself, he had no hesitation in arguing it for others (1 Cor 9:11-12; 2 Cor 11:7-9). Support of such workers makes us "fellow workers in the truth" (3 Jn 8).

In a day when one out of eight clergymen is resigning from the ministry, the church needs to be sensitive to the support of these servants. Certainly not all are resigning for financial reasons, but statistics show that this is a significant factor in many of their decisions to change professions. More than once a pastor has sat through a congregational meeting to hear the comment made, "But he's not really in it for the money." More often than not such a comment is a not so thinly disguised argument for "Let's pay him as little as we can get away with!"[5] Even in such ungracious and insensitive occasions, the Christian worker should model himself after the Apostle Paul. Do not demand your own rights, but demand the rights of others. For the congregation, the responsibility is the same. They must protect the right of the Christian worker to have sufficient support for his family. The question must be raised, "Are we paying a fair and just compensation for the service rendered?" The church is accountable for its compensation of the servant; the servant is accountable for the stewardship of that gift.

The converse of overpaid Christian workers is also a problem in some North American churches. Why is it that a pastor who works seventy hours a week in a congregation of two thousand is remunerated $35,000 and a fellow worker putting in equal time, though in a smaller church, makes $10,000? What biblical distinction is there between these two men? Why is one salary equivalent to that of a corporation director and the other to that of a street sweeper? Just because the average income of the church is higher does not mean that the worker must have that average. High salaries are often given because the congregation refuses to do the ministry and expects that a well-heeled professional will do it for them. "That's what we pay him for!" The pastor's salary can also be a balm to those who have guilty consciences over their love affair with money. Some adjustment in the system is necessary so that a man or woman is tempted neither to leave nor join the ministry for the money!

Something also needs to be said and done about provisions for Christian entertainers, writers and conference speakers. When an individual is invited to your church or city, sensitivity is as important as the remuneration. I have taken out-of-town conferences where people have been extremely hospitable. But there have also been times when no one has greeted me upon my arrival, no private place to be quiet and prepare talks has been offered, and no free time has been supplied from dawn till midnight. Every church needs its "prophet's chamber" where the itinerant can be at home away from home and have the sustenance for his work.

We need also to be concerned about the opposite extreme—the conference speaker or entertainer who commands $3,000 a night for a solo concert or talk, plus the most expensive hotels and meals in the city. The income of some of these people is astronomical. They may preach on the end of the world, but they have sunk their roots deep into the terra firma of this world. If Christians are going to face up to the demands of the kingdom, then we must do away with this wasteful, extravagant use of our resources.

Another priority of our Christian stewardship is to assist poor and needy Christians, both local and international. One of our elders recently returned from a trip to Washington, D.C. While there he spoke with Charles Colson, who now works in prison reform. Colson shared this story of his visit to an evangelical Bible college to speak at chapel. One young man in the front row took copious notes throughout the entire talk, highlighting certain comments with "Praise the Lord." When Colson got to the main point of his address, a concern for prison reform, the former admirer turned critic. Across the top of his note pad he wrote Social Gospel and immediately filed his notebook under the desk.

What a sad day when pockets of Bible-believing Christians still assume that concern for the poor and oppressed is a social gospel. There is only one gospel in the New Testament: the good news of God's Incarnation in his Son, to die a death on the cross, to rise triumphantly from the dead, and to proclaim salvation in his name. That is certainly the apex of God's revelation, but it is not the circumference. For the Lord Jesus on his road to Calvary fed the hungry, healed the sick and preached good news to those who would listen. Concern for the poor and needy Christians of this world is not a liberal or socialist concern; it's a biblical concern. If we believers in verbal, plenary, inerrant revelation would read the text, we would find that to be so. If we read Amos with Daniel, we would find it. If we read James with Revelation, we would find it there also.

Could it be that some of our thinking has become distorted in this area? For example, one popular eschatological system suggests that the worse things get, the better for us because the Lord's return is near. What comfort is this to a mother whose baby dies in her arms because of malnutrition? I'm talking about a born-again child of God, not someone who has never heard the good news about Jesus. And yet certainly our compassion should extend to unbelievers as well. Don't we need to repent of our blind eyes which cannot read the Scripture for what it says? Have we so encapsulated the Scripture within our economic and political conservatism that they have lost their impact on our lives? Just a few samplings from Scripture make God's concern for the poor abundantly clear:[6]

> Therefore I command you, You shall open wide your hand to your brother, to the needy and to the poor, in the land. (Deut 15:11)

> Blessed is he who considers the poor! The LORD delivers him in the day of trouble. (Ps 41:1)

> But when you give a feast, invite the poor, the maimed, the lame, the blind, and you will be blessed, because they cannot repay you. You will be repaid at the resurrection of the just. (Lk 14:13-14)

Only they would have us remember the poor, which very thing I was eager to do. (Gal 2:10)

If a brother or sister is ill-clad and in lack of daily food, and one of you says to them, "Go in peace, be warmed and filled," without giving them the things needed for the body, what does it profit? So faith by itself, if it has no works, is dead. (Jas 2:15-17)

Social gospel? Not in the least. This is the mandate the early church assumed. Because of its commitment to the poor, even its opponents said of them, "Behold, how they love one another." The church took care of its family and everyone noticed. The church answered with a resounding yes to the question, "Am I my brother's keeper?"

Some evangelicals view the plight of the poor like they do the oil crisis. "What oil crisis? I've still got gas for my car, don't I? So there must be no oil crisis." But the condition of the world's poor is real. We cannot stick our heads in the sand and pretend it does not exist. Statistics vary, but they are all overwhelming. More than ten thousand children five years of age and under die daily of malnutrition, more than one thousand in Latin America alone. Two billion people live in geographical areas with nutritional deficiencies. An estimated half of these suffer from recurrent crippling hunger. The lack of a balanced diet is as great a problem as the lack of food. Many simply do not get enough protein to exist.

Harold Kuhn, writing in *Christianity Today*, spoke most cogently to this problem and our wasteful habits: "Again it is difficult to understand the silence among the affluent Christians about the massive and perverse forms of waste; example, the annual rotting of 16 million tons (probably a conservative estimate) of cereal grains by the brewery and distilling industries in the United States. Or, scarcely less revolting, the grotesque and horrendous misuse of cereal grains and fish meat by the pet industry. Surely God whose heart beats with the hungry poor of the world must revolt with these senseless forms of waste. Surely some day, He will bring our nation along with other industrialized nations to judgment for the existence of these and similar forms of destruction of resources in an underfed and hungry world."[7]

Hunger is not the only problem. Polluted water and lack of adequate health care pose threats to life as well. Population experts tell us that the earth now holds four billion people. By the year 2000 we will be six billion and growing. The church of Jesus Christ must prepare to meet that growing need if it is to have credibility in the world. We say we worship a God of love who allowed the sacrifice of his own Son. How long will it be before the world clatters their empty cups and says, "Show us this God who would sacrifice for me"? Resource experts agree with Ghandi's statement that "there is a sufficiency in the world for man's need but not enough for man's greed." As the evangelical church of North America, heirs of a common Holy Spirit, are we not to expose the greed and covetousness which has been our bed partner? Is this not the day for a new sacrificial giving which will authenticate the integrity of the statement "God loves you"?

What's the Use?
Not long ago I received a picture commentary of the strife in Northern Ireland. Leon and Jill Uris, the authors of the book, summarized their feelings in an interview with an elderly Catholic man. This gentleman had witnessed the historic attempts at peace and could only conclude, "What's the use?" With one billion unreached by the gospel and two billion suffering from hunger and disease, there is a tendency by some evangelicals to ask the same question,

"What's the use?" Maybe this answer will prove helpful to you as it did to me.

Jesus does not call us to save the world as he did not call us to love the world. The task is too big. But he did ask us to love our neighbor. And who is our neighbor? The needy person God brings to our attention, no matter if that person is across the street, across the nation, or around the world. When God puts you on a collision course with a need, that is your neighbor.

Let me give you an example. In reading a missionary magazine several years ago, I spied an intriguing little article only four lines long. A missionary couple in Colombia had several children they wanted to place in Canadian homes. I placed the notice in our church newsletter and received response from several families. Two families pursued the matter and eventually brought home baby boys. As a church we have become financially and personally committed to the work in Colombia.

It is my conviction that God does not want us to bear the mental pressure for all the hungry children of the world. This would only lead us to further depression in face of such a hopeless task. However, I believe he wants us to be concerned for one child at a time as he brings them across our path. It may be children in the neighborhood whose mother works and is not able to give to them the emotional love so needed, or it may be the sponsoring of a child in a foreign country through one of the various Christian relief agencies, or even the adoption of an orphaned child, but it is one child at a time—loving our neighbor as ourself. We can't save the world or help the world. The task is too big. But we can be sensitive to neighbors who cross our path, in the parish and around the world. In a letter to *Time* magazine thanking them for their feature on twentieth-century saints, a reader wrote "I realize now the difference between me and them. I get emotional, saints get involved."

Affirmative Action

In this chapter and the last I have tried to show how Malachi's exhortation to financial stewardship and its development in Paul's letters can be applied to the church today. Let me summarize our findings.

1. Scripture says that God wants you before he wants your tithe. It also suggests that he has all of you when he has your tithe. For Christians in North America, ten per cent of their income (before taxes) is the minimum that should be released to the kingdom of God. This commitment should be regular and funneled primarily, though not exclusively, through the local church. Periodic giving beyond the tithe is also appropriate. This may be determined each month, or it may be on a set basis such as a graduated tithe. Ronald Sider has devised a program for a graduated tithe which adds a cumulative five-per-cent tithe to every $1,000 above your basic standard of living.[8]

2. Church budgets should be altered to reflect legitimate biblical concerns. For a start, I would suggest that the overall budget should show a commitment of at least fifty per cent of its resources for ministry outside the church. Of that amount, at least twenty-five per cent should be earmarked for foreign ministries. For churches with mortgage payments or for new churches which are struggling just to make ends meet, these percentages may be too severe. However, they can be goals toward which to work. Each year an increased percentage can be committed for outside ministries until the fifty-per-cent level is reached. Then there will be no reason to assume that we cannot or should not do more. The percentage levels I suggest are obviously relative and not fixed. However, biblical concerns must be reflected in our budgets as more than token items.

Our community has developed a threefold approach to monies going outside the church. First, we are committed to church planting throughout the world. We believe that

159

God's work is being done when converts are added to local fellowships. There they can grow in relationship to God and their fellow believers under the pastoral oversight of elders.

Next, we are committed to theological education. The church will not grow to maturity unless men and women are given opportunity to develop their pastoral and teaching skills. Not all these institutions are modeled after traditional Bible colleges or seminaries; some are innovative programs designed to reach people who have not had access to traditional schools.

Last, we support international social benevolences. This includes budgeted money for emergency relief projects such as the relocation of an Asian family or the restoring of a village devastated by an earthquake. There is also money for development programs. We have sponsored the digging of water wells in Haiti and the establishment of cottage industries in Bangladesh. At special times of the year we have given freewill offerings to worldwide ministries. At one Christmas, each member of the community was asked to forego one Christmas item and to give the money saved to a special fund. Part of the proceeds went to a prison ministry in Manila and the remainder to a children's camping ministry in Brazil.

3. Christians must halt their love affair with church buildings. Christians in the United States spent nearly six billion dollars on new church construction in the six years between 1967-72.[9] At the time, that was nearly $1.50 for every man, woman and child in the world. One church in our city is currently the record holder for a one-day building offering of two million dollars. I'm sure it will be quickly surpassed by another eager congregation. Every time I go past the place I want to faint. They already have one of the biggest facilities in the city. If the early church had needed buildings in order to grow, you and I would never have

been evangelized. But thank God they did not have that view. The church grew because Jesus was in the midst of his people, not in the midst of the building. We must resist the notion that the growth of the church is predicated on more and nicer church buildings.

4. We must put a check on our expanding lifestyle and learn to do more with less. A Quaker was leaning on his fence watching his new neighbor move in. After the movers had carted in all manner of fancy appliances, electronic gadgets, plush furniture and costly wall-hangings, the Quaker called over, "If you find you're lacking anything, neighbor, let me know and I will show you how to live without it."[10] Every North American Christian needs a Quaker living next door. There will be temptations to go back to full-throttled consumerism, but a church dedicated to a revised lifestyle can overcome these pressures.

Leighton Ford suggests beginning the "simple life" by asking four questions about everything you do or buy: "Will it have eternal and lasting significance? Will it clarify my spiritual vision? Will it make it easier to be devoted to Christ? Will it further God's kingdom?"[11]

While we work at simple lifestyles, we must also stay informed as to the needs of the world and how we could meet some of those needs. The church is to be committed to unlimited liability and total availability to the needs of Christians. We must "retain Jesus' distrust of wealth and avoid reducing the radical commands of Jesus into spiritual platitudes."[12]

5. We need to be patient with one another as we struggle in giving over economic control to Jesus. As a friend of mine once said, "If the devil can't get you by seducing you to wine, women and song, then he turns to be your accuser, often appearing as an angel of light in a clerical collar." Accusatory, guilt-laden, economic shibboleths from the pulpit will not change anyone. Each of us is at a differ-

ent point in seeing Jesus as Lord of our life. But let us not be afraid to confront those whose lives are possessed by covetousness. To fail to do so is to consign a soul to hell.

A man asked a friend if he knew the two greatest problems in the world. The friend responded, "I don't know and I don't care!" "You got them both," responded the man. Now we know some of the issues in economic stewardship. But the question remains, do we care? Have we been inundated with that Macedonian grace which allows us to give, even when we have needs ourselves? Or are we, as John Stott says, "allowing ourselves to become somewhat involved, enough to be responsible, but not enough to be uncomfortable"? The answer to that question is the litmus test of the evangelical church.

Six
O'Clock
in the
Evening

10

For months I had been praying that God would suddenly fill me with his Holy Spirit. On several occasions I had fallen asleep at my desk praying for this. I needed revitalization to overcome sinful behavior and to be able to minister to other people. Yet there seemed to be no answer. Then one morning I was invited to breakfast with a group of influential Christian leaders. As the meeting progressed it became quite apparent that the topic of conversation was to be yours truly. These brothers felt I needed correction for certain attitudes which I had exhibited during the previous month. Quite frankly, I felt like a pig being roasted over an open pit. I felt their criticisms deep to the bone. Childishly I reacted and began to trade insult for correction.

About this time a fourth brother entered the restaurant and sat down. I did not know at that moment but this friend had flown all night from Kansas City in order to be with me at breakfast. The night before, as he prayed and meditated, God specifically revealed to him that he was to be in Vancouver with me the next morning. As a faithful servant he had traveled all night to be with me. Arriving in town, he called my wife to find my whereabouts. She directed him to the breakfast meeting to which he drove immediately. There were only ten minutes of our meeting left when my friend arrived. Quietly he drank his juice and listened to the concluding comments. Needless to say, I was anxious to leave the moment the breakfast was over. I paid my bill and went straight to the car. My quiet and loyal friend followed along. Sitting silently in the car I was stunned by the previous hour. But my friend had not come just to be a comfort in my hour of need; he had brought a message from God.

As we prayed he said these words. "George, I believe God has a message for you in this. If God were to say it personally to you it would sound like this. 'George, you have prayed that I would fill you with my presence. I am now letting you know in a vivid way that I have done that. Coming to you, I will now refine every area of your life. There will be a purging of things intolerable. There will be a refining of things redeemable. Not one area shall escape my scrutiny, for I have begun a work in your life.' " I knew this to be God's word for me. I had expected a tremendous surge of power in my life with the filling of his Spirit, but it was rather the words of John the Baptist that came to mind. "He will baptize you with the Holy Spirit and with *fire*" (Mt 3:11).

Basilia Schlink, the spiritual spokeswoman of the Evangelical Sisterhood of Mary, describes the foundational premise of their ministry with these words. "God always works on us before using us as a channel of blessing for others."[1] There is much to suggest that both the evangelical and the charismatic sectors in North American Christianity are gaining considerable influence. The 1980s may be the doorway to a new Reformation. But with these positive signs, the Holy Spirit seems also to be saying to the church that refinement is a prerequisite of spiritual power.[2] Reformation does not come cheaply. We cannot expect to have revival and have it cost us nothing. Indeed it will cost us everything. It will cost us our egotism, our pride, our desire for self-advancement. There must be a purging of every thought that we may merit righteousness or deserve God's renewing touch. For a new Reformation in the church there must be an accent on God's cleansing activity. God's desire for his people remains what it was in Malachi's day. He longs to "purify the sons of Levi and refine them like gold and silver, till they present right offerings to the LORD. Then the offering of Judah and Jerusalem will be pleasing to the LORD as in the days of old and as in former years" (Mal 3:3-4).

Daddy Longlegs Is Loose

The Baptist preacher David Pawson is fond of speaking of the Holy Spirit as the Daddy Longlegs of the church.[3] *Daddy Longlegs* was a popular fictional story with a previous generation. It told of an orphan girl and her mysterious, anonymous benefactor. Only once in her life did she see him. On this occasion she was able to see only his shadow as it was distorted by the light in an alleyway. He appeared tall, thin and spidery, hence the name Daddy Longlegs.

For two thousand years the church of Jesus Christ has also had a benevolent Benefactor. But to many he is like Daddy Longlegs—distant, mysterious and anonymous. To some the very mention of his name strikes fear within their hearts.

This has not always been so. "Long before the Spirit was a theme of doctrine, He was a fact in the experience of the community."[4] Rather than being a proposition which one believed, he was a profound personal presence. Yet it did not take but a few years after Pentecost for the church to domesticate the Spirit of the living God. No longer was he a "roaring wind"; he was instead a "still quiet voice."

Thomas Aquinas, addressing Pope Innocent II, demonstrated the extent of the grieving process: Innocent had said, "The Church can no longer say silver and gold have we none." To which Aquinas retorted, "Neither can it say 'arise and walk.' "[5] The church in its desire for advancement and reputation had swapped the Spirit of God for the spirit of the age.

The Spirit's suppression was not always as severe as this suggests. At various times over the last nineteen hundred years the Holy Spirit has broken in to revive believers and convert nonbelievers. In our own day I believe this Benefactor is once again breaking loose in the midst of the church. In fact, some church historians and theologians suggest that the re-emergence of the Holy Spirit's power and gifts will be the most significant theme of twentieth-century church history.

However, the renewed outpouring of spiritual gifts has not been met without controversy. The polarity that has resulted is a great blight on the church. It is one of those areas in need of refinement. We cannot expect to march through the 1980s with any significant impact on our culture until there is essential harmony in our understanding of the Spirit's ministry, for a new Reformation will demand the Holy Spirit's empowering and refinement.

Wait for the Promise

John the Baptist was baptizing in the shallow waters of the Jordan when he announced his mandate for ministry and proclaimed a greater ministry to come. "As for me, I baptize you in water for repentance; but He who is coming after me is mightier than I, and I am not even fit to remove His sandals; He Himself will baptize you with the Holy Spirit and fire. And His winnowing fork is in His hand, and He will thoroughly clean His threshing floor; and He will gather His wheat into the barn, but He will burn up the chaff with unquenchable fire" (Mt 3:11-12 NASB). Before we attempt to define "baptism with the Holy Spirit," we need to provide a context for understanding the Spirit's ministry.

Before his ascension into heaven, Jesus told his disciples "to wait for what the Father had promised" (Acts 1:4 NASB). A promise is a verbal agreement given by God for the blessing of his people. Abraham was promised a great nation (Acts 7:17); Israel is promised a Savior (Acts 13:23); and the disciples of the Messiah were promised the Holy Spirit. In Acts 1—2, the promise is equated with the Holy Spirit.

The Holy Spirit had been promised in the Old Testament as part of the new covenant (Joel 2:28-32). Jesus made reference to this promise in the upper room when he spoke of giving his disciples "another Counselor" (Jn 14:16). In Greek there are two words used for "another." One word means "another of a different variety." The other word means "another of the same variety." It is this second word that Jesus uses on this occasion. The disciples were to be given another Jesus. A Spirit like him in substance and nature. In fact, so alike were they, they could be spoken of interchangeably. If his Spirit was in you, then Jesus was in you. If Jesus was in you, then his Spirit was in you. This One of the same substance and nature of the Lord Jesus would come and be with his people forever (Jn 14:15-28).

At this point there is often confusion. Where is Jesus Christ right this moment? In our evangelistic presentations we most often tell people that they must "receive Christ" or that Christ will come to live in their hearts. The phrase "Christ in you" (Col 1:27) is a biblical phrase; but Scripture repeatedly states that Jesus is ascended and seated at the right hand of the Father (Rom 8:34; Heb 1:3; 1 Pet 3:22; Rev 5:6). Scripture always places him in heaven at the Father's right hand having a ministry of intercession on our behalf. From his exalted position in heaven Jesus then manifests himself to us by his Spirit. The Holy Spirit comes and mediates Jesus to us. "When the Spirit of truth comes, he will guide you into all the truth; for he will not speak on his own authority, but whatever he hears he will speak, and he will declare to you the things that are to come. He will glorify me, for he will take what is mine and declare it to you" (Jn 16:13-14). Jesus is on his throne in heaven, but through the presence of his Holy Spirit he is present in every believer. Jesus Christ will not be real to us unless his Spirit is real to us, for it is the task of the Spirit to make Jesus present in our experience.

In similar fashion, to give ourselves to Jesus in commitment means that we give ourselves completely over to his Spirit, who in turn mediates our commitment to Jesus. There should be no conflict in our thinking between the Lord Jesus Christ and his Spirit. To say then that we need Jesus but not the Holy Spirit is not only theologically absurd but experientially arid.

With this background, what are we to make of the term "baptism of the Holy Spirit"? The term is much debated, and every sector of Christianity seems to define it with their own particular rigidity. Sacramentalists claim that the baptism of the Holy Spirit is that which we receive at our water baptism, Pentecostals maintain that it is an experience subsequent to conversion while evangelicals maintain that it is the watershed of one's conversion to Christ. The rigidity with which each group maintains its position reminds me of the young girl who asked her mother if God was in the room. The mother, trying to teach the nearness of God, said, "Yes, he's in the room." The little girl then asked if God was on the table on which she sat. The mother responded, "Yes, he's even there." Then the little girl said, "Is he in this milk bottle?" The mother, trying to convince the girl of the omnipresence of God, said, "Yes, even in the milk bottle." The little girl quickly placed her hand over the milk bottle and shouted triumphantly, "I've got him!"

A Bigger View

Both evangelicals and charismatics have had this arrogant attitude about the Spirit—"we've got him." However, Scripture will not tolerate such rigidity on any of our parts. Scripture gives us definite guidelines regarding what we should expect from the Holy Spirit, but with no sense of limiting his ministry. Michael Green has suggested that the term "baptism of the Holy Spirit" causes division because we do not define it large enough. I believe that an expanded understanding of the term should incorporate three different yet overlapping dimensions: the historical, the objective and the experiential.

The Historical Dimension. The baptism of the Holy Spirit has a historical dimension. The term itself is a bridge from the Gospels to the book of Acts. The ministry of the Spirit is foretold in the Gospels and is realized in Acts. Jesus, using the terminology of John the Baptist, associates the predictions of John with the day of Pentecost (Acts 1:5). "John baptized with water" but Jesus would "baptize with the Holy Spirit." Jesus began his ministry of baptizing with the Spirit on the day of Pentecost. "What Jordan was to Jesus," says James Dunn, "Pentecost was to the disciples. As Jesus entered a new age by being baptized by the Holy Spirit, so the disciples would follow Him at Pentecost."[6] Jesus the recipient of the Spirit became the Bestower of the Spirit.

The Objective Dimension. The baptism of the Holy Spirit also has an objective dimension. In 1 Corinthians 12:13 Paul describes Spirit-baptism as the sovereign act of God which initiates us into the body of Christ. Two pictures come from this verse. The first is the action of the Spirit as he places us into one body. We are baptized into or engulfed by that body. The second picture is of imbibing the Spirit. All believers in Christ have been "made to drink of one Spirit." If we have not drunk of the Spirit or been placed into the body, then we are not Christ's (Rom 8:9).

Paul is appealing to an empirical fact which needed to be understood by the divided Corinthians. He is not so much concerned with the emotion or manifestation that accompanied this incorporation as with the doctrinal conception that all the Corinthians have been given God's Spirit and have been placed into one family. In Paul's language the baptism of the Spirit occurs when we come to know Jesus. It is not an act subsequent to conversion. He maintains that there is only one baptism in the Spirit (Eph 4:3), but many fillings (Eph 5:18).

It is unfortunate that some today maintain the use of this term as a postconversion experience. This only causes unnecessary confusion regarding conversion. At the same time it can be said that evangelicals are generally unaware that many charismatics have also avoided this term. These charismatics are much more comfortable with terms like "filling of the Spirit" or the "release of the Spirit."[7]

The Experiential Dimension. Finally, the baptism of the Holy Spirit has an experiential dimension. It is at this point that evangelicals usually get into a flap. This is because we have become so Paul-oriented that we fail to consider what other biblical texts say on the subject of Spirit-baptism. We want to read Luke as though he were Paul. But the authoritative diversity of Holy Scripture maintains that Paul must be Paul and Luke must be Luke.

In Paul, baptism of the Spirit is incorporation into the body of Christ at conversion. However, when we come to Luke, we find that he is not so much concerned with the *time* of the event as with the *nature* and *purpose* of the baptism (Acts 1:8; 2:4, 11). For him, to be baptized in the Spirit is to have the dynamic experience of being enveloped in the Holy Spirit. It is an encounter where Jesus immerses us in himself. This is no mere objective statement but an overwhelming experience.

The purpose of baptism on the day of Pentecost was to launch a new dispensation. It was a day when God's Spirit was poured out on all humanity in order that men and women might have power to witness the prophetic message of God (Acts 2:1-21). In Paul, Spirit-baptism is for incorporation. For Luke, Spirit-baptism is for the enabling of mission.

If we are going to remain faithful to the intent and purpose of all of Scripture, then we must understand this term within the full scope Scripture calls for. As Clark Pinnock has said, " 'Baptism' is a flexible metaphor, not a technical term. Luke seems to regard it as synonymous with 'fullness' (Acts 2:4; cf. 11-16). Therefore, so long as we recognize conversion as truly a baptism in the Spirit, there is no reason why we cannot use 'baptism' to refer to subsequent fillings of the Spirit as well. The later experience, or experiences, should not be tied in with the tight 'second blessing' schema, but should be seen as an *actualization* of what we have already received in the initial charismatic experience, which is conversion."[8]

Evangelicals need to exercise greater patience with those who claim they have had a postconversion baptism in the Spirit. We need to be more concerned over the nurturing of this filling than correcting certain words which describe the experience. I have discovered that if I encourage people in their fresh walk with God, sooner or later I will be able to share with them the theological structure which undergirds renewal in the Spirit. For the moment though, I am to rejoice with them in this fresh inundation of Christ's presence.

Evangelicals have tended to emphasize the *objective* dimension of the baptism while Pentecostals have emphasized the *experiential*. But we must not allow these to be divided. A wedding makes you married, but it is not what makes up the day-to-day experience of marriage. "I do" may make you married, but it does not keep you in love. We have been married to Christ by the work of his Spirit, but we cannot let it go there. We must constantly be inundated by his Spirit in order to remain in love.

The Happy Hustler

At one time or another all of us have been accosted by a pentecostal happy hustler. This person wants to revitalize our sleepy, lifeless, secure, orthodox Christianity. They accuse us of being Pepsis without any fizz, flat-tire versions of Christianity. Quite frankly, their analysis is often correct. Evangelicals have always assumed that they "got it all in conversion" and therefore were in need of no more. But as Martyn Lloyd-Jones once pointed out, "If we've got it all, why are we as we are?"

Over the last few years I have traveled to a number of student conferences. At some evangelical student meetings I often find many who are more interested in recreation than in prayer, worship, Bible study, evangelism and discipleship. At charismatic student conferences, on the other hand, I have found many who wanted nothing more than to pray, worship and study the Scriptures.

As evangelicals, we have no option but to confess our great need for revitalization in the Holy Spirit. However, I would maintain that it is wrong to say that we need a second baptism. We need a release of that same dynamic which first placed us into Christ Jesus. Paul declares that we have been blessed "in Christ with every spiritual blessing in the heavenly places (Eph 1:3). Therefore, we need a release of all that is ours in Christ Jesus. We must halt our grieving and quenching the Spirit and let him work in our lives as he chooses. D. L. Moody once said, "I believe in the

filling of the Holy Spirit, but I also believe you can leak."
Sealed and baptized people do leak. We quench and grieve
the power of the Holy Spirit (Eph 4:30; 1 Thess 5:19);
therefore we need continually to turn back to God and to
receive all the fullness of his presence (Eph 5:18).

It is not sufficient to sit back with an objective understanding of the baptism of the Spirit. We are to enter every
blessing which God has given us in Christ Jesus. In our commitment to doctrinal integrity we have often exaggerated
what we think and have underrated what we are experiencing. It is easy from this position to slip into an attitude of
being perfected in the flesh without reliance on the Spirit.
But in the same manner we began with Christ—that is, by
faith and the Spirit—we are to continue our walk, in order
that the Spirit of God might do his sanctifying work in our
lives (Gal 3:2-3).

Although there are still pockets of harsh resistance and
negative criticism, many Christians are coming to Jesus
Christ and asking for a fresh bestowal of all that is theirs
in Christ. In unique ways, fitted to individual personalities,
God's Spirit is breathing a fresh revitalization into lives and
churches. Contrary to classical Pentecostal theology, which
demands the uniformity of speaking in tongues as a sign of
the Spirit's presence, there seems to be no set pattern in
what God's Spirit is doing in his people. Revitalized, these
Christians are manifesting more fully the fruit of the Holy
Spirit. Likewise, gifts and ministries are also more evident.
In some cases, the gift of tongues or prophecy is being
exercised. Although these gifts may bring great elation to
the person, they are only two of a wide diversity of gifts
given to Spirit-filled people.

In his book *Reflected Glory,* Tom Smail makes clear that
the experience of being filled with the Holy Spirit will
be different for each believer. Yet there will be a common
ingredient, the realization that the Spirit has come and is

now working in our lives. "It may be sudden, critical and sensationally transforming; it may be slow and quiet and spread over a period; the Spirit is symbolized by dew and by wind, but even when the dew falls, silently, it will make the leaves wet and fresh and sweet. Even when the Spirit comes quietly we shall be aware that He has come, and His manifestation will be known also in the body of Christ around us."[9] We only do great pastoral damage in maintaining a rigid stereotype of the Spirit's filling. The breath of God and the image of God in man mix as new ingredients in every believer.

Help, There's a Charismatic in My Bedroom

I have seen this diversity of experience even in my own home. My wife had been a Christian for almost twenty years when she began to notice an aridity in her walk with Jesus Christ. She had exercised a disciplined life of quiet time and prayer for those years, yet she was struggling for a more intimate knowledge of God's presence. As a good evangelical she had sublimated many of her mystical desires in reading C. S. Lewis and J. R. R. Tolkien. Yet none of these was able to meet the fullest need of her heart. One day, while she was interceding for me, God suddenly released upon her the very presence of his Spirit. There came a new freshness and vigor in her life. She spoke in a language which she did not know. Looking back now, she recognizes this as a decisive moment of renewal.

What was my first reaction to this revitalization? Intimidation! Here I was, the teaching elder of a church with a wife whose enthusiasm and affection for Jesus Christ far outpaced my own. For the next year there was a great deal of controversy within our home. I tried to maintain my evangelical cool, giving counterpoint answer to every suggestion she made. But she had been schooled in the same tradition as I had been and was committed to a proper doctrinal understanding of the Spirit. I could not refute her doctrinally, for she was saying what we had always believed, but her renewed experience posed a point of tension.

Finally, after a year of personal intimidation I began to reflect on my own relationship to the Spirit. Week after week I sorted through negative attitudes and reactions. I then found myself thirsting and hungering for greater assurance of God's presence with me. As I read his Word daily, it assured me that he wanted to have an intimate relationship with me. But for me, the filling of his spirit was never sudden, critical and sensationally transforming. My experience was slow and spread out over several years. Yet, in retrospect, there is no doubt that the Spirit of God had begun to work. His fruits were produced to a greater extent. Gifts, some of which I had never experienced before, and far different from my wife's, began to manifest themselves. There was no doubt that I was experiencing a renewal of my initial baptism into Christ. Some may read this section as charismatic testimony in evangelical clothing. But it is possible to be thoroughly evangelical in one's exegesis and doctrine and to be revitalized in the Holy Spirit. As long as one does not preclude what gifts God can give to his church today and assumes that God wants to reveal himself to us, then there can be a revitalization of our sterile orthodoxy.

Evangelicals have been so concerned about proper terminology that we have failed to foster a healthy experience of being filled with the Holy Spirit. Therefore, in mentioning the ministry of the Holy Spirit one is often branded a pentecostal. But, let us not give the ministry of the Holy Spirit over exclusively to those who are called charismatics or pentecostals. The Holy Spirit of God does not discriminate on the basis of labels. He is ready to work in any heart which is fully open.

Taking the Plunge

To be filled with the Holy Spirit one must come to Jesus in the same manner in which he came in salvation, by faith. We must come acknowledging the need of his work in our life. We must repent of the Laodicean heresy, the self-sufficiency which claimed, "I am rich, I have prospered, and I need nothing" (Rev 3:17). We must see that we are miserable and blind and naked without Christ's continuing work in our lives. So we simply come and ask Jesus to fill our thirsty vessels. "If any one thirst, let him come to me and drink. He who believes in me, as the scripture has said, 'Out of his heart shall flow rivers of living water.' Now this he said about the Spirit, which those who believed in him were to receive; for as yet the Spirit had not been given, because Jesus was not yet glorified" (Jn 7:37-39).

Canadian journalist Peter Newman tells the story of his first experience covering a news event in the Maritime provinces. Trying to make small talk with one of the farmers, he inquired, "Have you lived here all your life?" The farmer thought for a moment and replied, "No, not yet." Newman was expecting an answer that reflected the man's past, but the man gave an answer looking toward his future. This is the way we ought to describe our experience of the Holy Spirit. A simple "I found it" ignores the dynamic adventures yet to come. We need to talk more of what there is yet to discover than of what we have already uncovered. To the question "Do you know the Holy Spirit?" we should want to respond, "No, not fully."

Gossiping Jesus Wherever You Go

When Christ's Spirit gains control of our lives there are two things he will want to do. First, he will lead us to bear witness to Jesus Christ. "But you shall receive power when the Holy Spirit has come upon you; and you shall be my witnesses in Jerusalem and in all Judea and Samaria and to the end of the earth" (Acts 1:8). The Spirit does not come for our own personal enjoyment. The Spirit of God is a missionary Spirit, sending us out to witness for Christ.

For many of us the Lord's promise of power in witness seems unfulfilled. We imagine that we should become dynamic evangelists able to persuade masses with the gospel message. But our expectation misses the essential ingredient of the passage. What does it mean that we "shall receive power"?

What do you expect will happen? Do you envision a new personality invading your old body, infusing it with dynamic ability? Too often this is what we expect. The word *power,* in Greek or in English, has as its root meaning the idea of capacity or ability, not necessarily great force or strength. What is promised here is the ability to overcome our natural inclination to hide under a basket (Mt 5:15). We are promised that we will be made able to press beyond our fears of sharing Christ with others. We will not necessarily become great "soul winners," but we will become more like the Christians of the early church. We should find ourselves more freely talking about Jesus wherever we are. When the Spirit of God has revitalized the presence of Jesus in us, we cannot help but speak his name in normal conversation. This strategy more than anything else turned the world upside-down for Christ (Acts 17:6).

Not all of us have evangelistic gifts. One evangelist friend of mine estimates that only one in ten Christians has the gift of evangelism, so few members of the body of Christ will find evangelism to be their primary ministry. But all members of the body of Christ will be able to "be witnesses" because Jesus Christ has filled their lives.

The significance of the promise of Acts 1:8 came home to me in 1971. I was one of several speakers for a campus mission at the University of Texas. We had decided to do open-air preaching during the lunch hour. Thousands of students would be filing through the central plaza of the University, and it was an appropriate place for sharing the message of Christ. We drew straws to see who should be the first speaker. The lot fell to me. I had done outdoor preaching on several occasions, but this time I was petrified. A number of Christians gathered with me to pray. As they prayed I soon sensed that the fear was leaving. In its place there was internal desire to share Jesus Christ. My performance that day certainly would not be recorded as a great and powerful evangelistic sermon, but I was *able* to stand up and share the message. Not a human dynamo with powerful persuasion, but *enabled* by the Spirit to share God's love.

The Refiner's Fire
The second ministry of the Holy Spirit is to conform us to the image of Christ (Rom 8:29; 2 Cor 3:18). Those who believe that the Holy Spirit is given only for personal joy and power have heard only half of the story. They may have read Dennis Bennett's *Nine O'Clock in the Morning* with its emphasis on renewal, but a new book needs to be written, *Six O'Clock in the Evening*, which would deal with the ongoing refinement of God's Spirit.[10] Richard Lovelace accents this point when he says,

> Any model of the fullness of the Spirit which attempts to make empowering for service relatively separate from growth in holiness inevitably collides with the truth represented in the very title *Holy Spirit*. The principal work of the Spirit in applying redemption lies in making us holy, and being filled with the Spirit simply means having all our faculties under his control rather than under the control of sin.[11]

John the Baptist announced that Jesus would come baptizing with the Holy Spirit and with fire (Mt 3:11; Lk 3:16). John, taking his cue from Malachi, spoke of a consuming fire which would destroy the wicked yet purify the righteous. Charles Hummel suggests that "John's statement apparently indicates that the *same* persons ("you") are to be baptized with both the Spirit and fire. Therefore it is probable that for the disciples the fire refers to the purifying power of the Messiah's baptism."[12] The picture is seen vividly in the tongues of fire which hover over the believers on the day of Pentecost. Not only were they enabled to witness, but their lives were never the same.

When the Spirit comes he is like the character in Shaw's Pygmalion "who will decorate our home from cellar to dome, and then go on with the enthralling fun of overhauling you." Again, as we have said before, "God loves us the way we are, but he loves us too much to leave us that way." Therefore he sends his refining Spirit to purge us of all our sinful behavior in order that our characters might be conformed to the image of Christ.

Jesus, at the right hand of the Father, reveals himself to us through the Spirit. The Spirit, mediating the presence of Jesus, reveals to us the glory of God's character. Such revelation causes us to reflect on the inadequacy of our own lives, especially because we now desire "to be like him." That desire, coupled with the enablement of the Spirit, leads us on in the transformation process. We begin to take on the fruits of Christ and the character of Christ in order to do the work of Christ.

It is not an easy road to follow. Every turn reveals new layers of carnality which we never dreamed to be possible. But thankfully, the Spirit's touch transforms rather than destroys. Personally, I am very grateful to God for these past few years. I thought I needed power, but I really needed subduing. I wanted great victories, but God thought it better that I have some quiet polishing. At last I can say appreciatively that he knows exactly what he is doing.

Thanks, Lord, I Really Needed That

11

My first three years out of university I served on the campus staff of Inter-Varsity Christian Fellowship. This meant that I moved from campus to campus, traveling three to four days a week. Often I stayed with Christian families. At first I accepted any invitation for bed and breakfast, but as time went on I began to choose my lodging more carefully. There were two things that affected my choice. First was bedding. I quickly realized that for my body a soft mattress led to back pain the next morning. Second was parent-child relationships. Newly married and without children of my own, I nevertheless had some definite ideas about child rearing.

Let me describe for you two models I observed. Model one was "blind parent and assaulting child." Two minutes after entering the door I was verbally and physically abused by a preschool delinquent. The parent sat there with an apparently blind eye to the whole episode. My gut reaction was to turn a guided muscle loose on the child's face. Knowing that this would do my public relations no good, I simply seethed under the tension. When I got home I barked to my wife, "I'm really going to sock it to *our* children if they don't behave."

The second model was "explosive parent and quivering child." Greeted at the door with a Marabel Morgan smile, I was served coffee and told to have a seat. Johnny, off in a corner, had quietly taken for himself milk from the refrigerator. But the door was still ajar. The mother told the child to shut the door, but as so often happens the child did not hear enough to obey. A rumble began at the table. One could see that an eruption was about to take place. Finally the dam broke. The child in holy panic attempted to close the refrigerator door. From sheer embarrassment I conveniently hid myself in the bread box. Arriving home I said to my wife, "Being angry with your children is very destructive." These and a multitude of other examples led me to the conclusion that I had to study the biblical concept of discipline in order to understand my walk with God and to be a good father.

As I said in the previous chapter, the baptism of the Holy Spirit is not only for power but also for refinement. But how does the Spirit work in conforming us to Christ? What is the process used by this Refiner with his fire, this laundryman with his soap (Mal 3:2)? I think the answer is found in the biblical doctrine of discipline. There are various New Testament words which describe this same process; trials and testing (Jas 1), afflictions (2 Cor 1), tribulations (Rom 12:12) and suffering (1 Pet 2:18-25). However, the most thoroughly explained of all these terms is the word *discipline*.

For some reason, in my mind discipline had always been synonymous with punishment. I suppose the lingering idea of "chastisement" from the KJV had led me to this conclusion. But as I began to read the Scriptures on discipline I found they talked more about education than punishment. Paul uses this word to describe the instruction of children (Eph 6:4) and Luke uses it of Paul's schooling under Gamaliel (Acts 22:3). Though punishing a deviant student might occasionally be the last resort of a teacher, the primary concern of discipline is the education of the student. It is not punishment but refinement which is God's main concern. Hebrews 12 presents to us a detailed analysis of God's refining process. It describes the loving incentives used by God to create his image in us. Jesus is our model. The Holy Spirit is our tutor. We are to be refined into a life which conforms to Christ.

Fix Your Eyes on Jesus

Even Jesus himself endured the refining process (Heb 12:2-3). If you associate discipline with punishment, then you will have a difficult time discovering the wrongdoing for which Jesus was punished. Certainly Jesus bore the wrath of our sin on the cross (1 Pet 2:24; Is 53:5) but the hostility the author of Hebrews refers to occurred prior to the cross. The implication is that God the Father disciplined Jesus by letting him suffer at the hands of hostile men (Mt 4:1; 10:24-25; 11:19; 12:14; 16:1; 21:38; 22:15; 26:48, 59, 69-70; 27:29-31) in order that he might have the experience of trusting God in difficult moments. It is through this that the Son of God learned obedience (Heb 5:8).

Rising from the Jordan waters full of the Holy Spirit, he was immediately led into a period of testing (Mk. 1:9-13). But this was just the first phase of a series of tests, ending with the crucifixion, that he had to undergo before he was raised into heaven as the exalted Son of God.

Alan Paton, in his book *Cry, the Beloved Country,* has written, "I have never thought that a Christian would be free of suffering. For our Lord suffered. And I have come to believe that He suffered, not to save us from suffering, but to teach us how to bear suffering. For He knew that there is no life without suffering."[1] This word challenges the triumphant spirit in evangelical and charismatic circles today. Yet the point is scarcely understood.

Several years ago the well-known German pastor and theologian Helmut Thielicke toured the United States. He was asked to name the greatest defect among American Christians. He replied, "The inadequate view of suffering." The view of suffering which suggests that we can expel it by faith or grin and bear it fails to comprehend the degree to which God wants to work in our lives. If Jesus himself endured discipline and learned obedience, then his disciples must be prepared to do likewise.

While working on a ranch one summer I saw the wrangler take a two-by-four and hit one of the horses on the head. I wasn't sure what was going on. Later he told me that it was the only way of getting the horse's attention. Sometimes, God must hit us on the head to get our attention. He wants to move us along in our education but he cannot get us to listen. Our lives are so bound by activities that we seldom slow down to hear him speak. Occasionally God must break through these barriers to let us know how seriously he considers our education to be. As C. S. Lewis has said, "Suffering is a megaphone to arouse a deaf world." God wants us to wake up, to clean the wax from our ears and to take seriously his intervention in our lives.

While I was writing this book I went through long bouts of physical pain. At first it was just a nuisance which I thought would disappear. But soon it began to drain my strength and distract from my work. Some friends recommended that I could get rid of the problem by active faith. Others suggested that I should just grin and bear it. But God seemed to be saying that this was his way of getting my attention in order to tell me some things about myself. A year and a half later, the pain lessened. Although it did not all go away, I realized some invaluable lessons about myself. As I said in the previous chapter, I wanted power but God wants refinement.

This educational process, though it may appear to come from an evil source, ultimately emanates from the hand of God. To think otherwise is to agree that evil wins over good, and that evil forces are sovereignly in control and not God.

Once, while traveling in New Zealand, I fell ill simultaneously with the flu and an allergic drug reaction. I lay in bed for five days, being visited by my doctor three times a day. The sickness came at a focal point of the trip and was quickly analyzed by many of the elders to be spiritual warfare. There were moments during the sickness when I was delirious. I began to hallucinate, thinking I was hearing God's voice. But it was the enemy leading me into confusion. Satan had loosed his army on my body and mind to keep me from my work. As we prayed, we had the confident expectation that God was in control, that he was the Triumphant One over evil. By the end of the week I was able to muster the strength to attend the conference. The opening song for the weekend rang out, "He is Lord. He is Lord. He is risen from the dead and he is Lord." As the congregation began to sing I broke down in great sobbing tears. Uncontrollably, I cried for five minutes. When I gained my composure I clearly realized that the battle had been won. Satan had been defeated; God was in control. I was raised up to minister through the course of the weekend. It was the greatest learning experience I have had in the ministry. Though evil forces were loose, God harnessed them for his own purpose.

I was shocked to read this comment in a notable theological dictionary: "The contradiction between God's justice and mercy still remains. Even the idea of chastisement of love cannot resolve it."[2] But to say this is to suggest that God is either not all good or not all powerful. Though it strains our imagination Scripture nevertheless affirms that he is both. He loves us and takes a vested interest in our education. He is in control of our refinement and his love permits these interventions.

Quite frankly, we often feel, "Lord, please don't love me quite so much. I don't want to be greedy and take so much. Please feel free to spread it around." This feeling usually grows out of our desire to be a "love child" rather than a "loved child." We would rather be pampered and spoiled than matured by love. But let us not doubt that God is more concerned with our refinement than our pleasure.

Discipline and Disobedience

Though the primary emphasis is on education, inherent within the concept of discipline is the idea of correction (Prov 13:24; 22:15; 23:13). The rabbis did not shy from suggesting that God spanked Israel for their rebellion. He purged their sin that they might turn around in their behavior.

In the Old Testament it was assumed as a working principle that suffering derived from sin. Rewards were to come in this life; therefore any deprivation was due to personal sin. Job's counselors made this principle a rigid rule and tried to foist it on Job (8:1-7). They wanted him to take his medicine, though he maintained his innocence throughout. These friends were legalists of the Old Testament. They had a simple, rigid rule for every problem. But as you know, they were completely unaware that Satan, with God's permission, was really the source of the suffering.

In the New Testament the principle of suffering because of sin takes a back seat to the premise that suffering and testing are part of God's means to produce character (1 Pet 1:6-7). Suffering may still be due to disobedience (Ps 39:11; 1 Cor 11:30; Jas 5:16). In such cases, there must be confession of wrongdoing, restitution where necessary and the settled conviction to turn around one's behavior. Then, and only then, will the hand of God be lifted.

However, it is also possible that God is allowing such suffering to produce character in our lives. The question "Why is this happening to me?" can only occasionally be answered directly. Here again we must be careful that we are not functioning with the rigidity of Job's friends. We must also remember that Jesus, though innocent and righteous, still suffered. On some occasions we do not know why we were meant to endure such pressures. We can only trust that a sovereign God is working out his plan in our life. God never really answers the question why in Job's case. He simply suggests that suffering produces invaluable qualities. Sometimes we recognize those qualities. Then the message of suffering is clear.

At other times we may not be aware of what is being produced. Suffering may have a message, but we are not sure what it is. Then our concentration should be not on the *why* but on the *how* of coping with our situation.

Peter in his epistle to scattered and suffering Christians urges them to rejoice, not because it is pleasurable, but because it is productive (1 Pet 4:13). Rejoice because you have an opportunity to walk in the same steps that Jesus trod. The church throughout history has consistently viewed suffering as a high calling in the service of Jesus Christ.

Peter also urges his readers to entrust their souls to a faithful Creator (1 Pet 4:19). Though Job had no complete answer for his suffering, in the last chapter he gets a picture of who God is. This breaks in like sun dispelling the morning mist. With his enlarged view of God he can trust though he still does not fully understand his suffering.

Finally, Peter urges those who suffer to continue to do good (1 Pet 4:19). Suffering can be used as a pretext for disobedience. "It hurts too much, it's too painful, it's too hard to obey, therefore I will not." I have been trying to teach my young son this lesson. First ventures on a bicycle are bound to bring bumps and cuts. They also bring un- controllable tears and the assumption that since he is hurt he need no longer obey the ground rules. But the sympathy my son needs is not a relaxing of the ground rules, but encouragement and help in developing a spirit of perse- verance through difficult circumstances. Although we hurt, we are still to do the good.

Refinement Is for All

In case we are a little smug about our piety and think we can avoid God's discipline by being good, it's important that we realize that all of us receive God's refinement. There are no double promotions in God's educational sys- tem. If you do not receive an indication of God's refining, it is not a question of a special dispensation for you, but a question of whether or not you are his son or daughter. Discipline guarantees our sonship.

I often retreat to a Catholic monastery to pray and study. The Benedictine monks who run the monastery are an order dedicated to prayer and worship. There is always absolute silence during the eating of our meals. One day when entering the dining hall I noticed at the end table a huge sign in red letters which said "Quiet." Humorously I chuckled under my breath that even these highly disci- plined brothers occasionally needed a practical reminder from their abbot. All of us need God's education. No one is immune from the process.

The author of Hebrews encourages his readers to "strive for . . . the holiness without which no one will see the Lord" (12:14). The holiness he has in mind is not just the judicial rendering in which God declares us to be righteous, but the holy life which is produced in us as we "walk in the light" (1 Jn 1:7). Holiness comes as we grow with God. God uses all means to sanctify his people. His resources are endless. He uses our children, our work, our bodies, our spouses, our enemies and our friends to produce in us a holy life.

At the Urbana Missionary Conference in 1976 Elisabeth Elliot shared with the audience a visit she had with Corrie ten Boom:

As she talked about her own experience and that of my husband Jim, she took out a piece of embroidery which she held with the back to us—just as a jumble of threads that made no sense at all. She repeated for us this poem:

My life is but a weaving betwixt my God and me,
I do not choose the colors, he worketh steadily.
Oftimes He weaveth sorrow, and I in foolish pride,
Forget He sees the upper and I the underside.

She then turned the piece over and we saw that it was a gold crown on a purple background.[3]

Our lives often appear to be a jumble of threads. We feel like an onion which is constantly being peeled and exposed layer after layer. Yet it is what God is doing with the embroidery which should be our concern. He's taking these scattered occasions of hostility, suffering, testing and temptation and drawing them into a pattern which will produce in us sanctification.

We live in a generation which believes that all discipline is administered unjustly. Discipline is associated with vindictive personalities. In one report issued during the International Year of the Child there was the suggestion that "all spanking is really child beating." No doubt, capricious and inconsistent parenting has brought about this misconception. Parents usually take action in what they believe to be the child's best interest. Sometimes they are right, other times wrong. But God assures us that he is always working for our good. He is not like an earthly father who disciplines without cause. He is concerned. He is methodical. And he is dedicated to our own good.

Responding to Refinement
The author of Hebrews says that all discipline seems painful for the moment (12:11). The educational process will occasionally produce great sorrow in our lives. There are two responses that we can have. First, we can know that God has allowed this event to transpire in our life, coming through the loving filter of his sovereign hand. Although there may be immediate sorrow, eventually it will produce a peaceful fruit of righteousness. Or, second, we can allow sorrow to overwhelm us and lead us into unbelief (Heb 12:15). Instead of seeing a good and sovereign God we can become bitter and angry. Construing discipline as a means of destroying our lives, we may fail to see the constructive aspect of the test. This bitterness can be passed on to our children and to the church if it is not effectively dealt with.

God intends no believer to go it alone through the refining process. As Bonhoeffer says, "It is infinitely easier to suffer with others than to suffer alone." Weakness is characteristic of our experience in the refining process. We need one another to hold up weak limbs, to help put what is out of joint in place. In a weak and vulnerable moment we will be tempted like Esau to sell our birthright for short-term gain. It is then that the body of Christ must minister to us, not letting us fall into temptation but helping us through the test.

We must allow others to come and minister to us in these suffering moments. The natural tendency is to seek seclusion. In seclusion we lick our own wounds. Self-sorrow provides fertile soil for unbelief. Some Christians live life in a terrarium, trying to get along without any outside help. We comfort ourselves singing "Nobody knows the trouble I've seen, nobody knows but Jesus." But the Bible indicates that refinement is something that we are never meant to do alone. In fact, the pain and tension are often diminished as they are absorbed by the community.

Sometimes, however, friends pose the greatest difficulty in our suffering. Job found this out quickly. No sooner had trouble come than he was hounded by his friends to swallow his own medicine. "If you believe sinners suffer then stop pretending you're so good." At the end of the story Job must forgive his friends before his fortunes are restored.

Peter gives us some sound advice for dealing with suffering friends. First, we are to exercise sound judgment (1 Pet 4:7). We are to be reasonable and sensible with one another. We are not to get so emotionally empathetic that we become a worry to the person. We are to be self-restrained in order to pray. We are not to let our own ideas get in the way of our prayers. We must listen to what the Spirit of God is saying regarding our counsel and encouragement.

We also need to love one another because love covers a multitude of sin (1 Pet 4:8). Suffering people are people who are not their normal selves. They do things they would not normally do. They may be grumpy and on edge with nervous habits. They might be easily hurt. All of these abnormal attitudes and actions must be absorbed by loving forgiveness. Practically, we are to go out of our way to show hospitality. We are to do this without complaining (1 Pet 4:9).

Last, we are to serve people in their dilemmas with our charismatic self (1 Pet 4:10-11). We are to offer them the gifts that God wants to give through us. It is not simply running off at the mouth or merely busying ourselves, but providing people with services that God the Spirit has inspired.

Ray Stedman once defined a Christian as one who is "completely fearless, continually cheerful and constantly in trouble." If not in trouble, at least in the process of refinement. Every trial comes for our own good and is meant to be turned into an altar for worship.

Joni Eareckson, speaking of her own quadriplegic paralysis as a "momentary light affliction" in preparation for God's full plan, exemplifies this attitude. Horatio Spafford displayed it, too. Spafford lost seven children and his wife in a shipping disaster while on their way to Jerusalem. Later when returning by ship the captain spoke to him of the exact location where his wife and children had gone down. Retreating to his room he penned these words. "When peace like a river attendeth my way, When sorrows like sea billows roll; Whatever my lot, Thou hast taught me to say, 'It is well, it is well with my soul.'" These two have learned the secret of giving thanks in everything (1 Thess 5:18). It hurts, but it helps. We go through the process thanking Jesus that nothing comes in our direction lest it come through his protective hand and that everything that eventually reaches us comes for our education and refinement.

Same Old Group of People?

The story is told of a church which burnt down and had no place for the congregation to meet. The only facility available on a Sunday morning was the local saloon. This saloon contained a loquacious parrot who constantly kept the patrons entertained. On the first Sunday morning of the congregational meeting the parrot sat quiet through most of the service. However, during one of the silent moments of reflection he brought forth his interpretation of the morning, "Err, new bartender. Err, new piano player. Err, same old group of people."

Will the church remain the same old group of people? Can we enter the Christian faith and live in the Christian community and not be radically different from the world? God has elected from the beginning of creation to separate a people who would glorify his name. He desires that his name be great among the nations. To accomplish this he has chosen to refine a people to glorify that name. God's very reputation is at stake. The failure of people to be refined jeopardizes the whole kingdom of God. So it is his intention to work personally in each believer and corporately in the whole gamut of family and intercommunity relationships. Not only will he rearrange our personal lives, but he will also rearrange our corporate and institutional structures. It is through the church the manifold wisdom of God is made known to principalities and powers, and God intends to see that the church is sufficiently refined to make known his wisdom.

The Need of the Eighties

His six-foot-three frame, long blond hair and hippie attire stood at the end of my sick bed. Although he had only been converted a few months, I knew from the moment he opened his mouth that God sent him to me. I mustered all my strength to listen to what he had to say. His message was simple and direct; there was no mistaking its intention. "George, God is saying to the church that she looks like a prostitute. He will not allow her to continue following after other gods. He has begun a process of refinement. He will not conclude that refinement until the bride is made perfectly clean for the wedding feast. God had said that the church must be cleansed."

The prophet Jeremiah could not have said it any more profoundly. Although this incident transpired during the days of the Jesus movement, it is not a word the church can ignore if it is to have the ministry God wants for it in the 1980s. The renewal of the church may be within grasp for those who are prepared not only to be empowered by the Spirit but also to be refined by the Spirit.

May our prayer be that of the early church as recorded in the Didache.

Lord,

193

Remember your Church.
Rescue it from all evil
and perfect it in your love.

And gather it, the sanctified one, from the four winds into your
Kingdom which you have prepared for it. For power and glory
are yours forever.[4]

Notes

Preface
[1]Two books were most helpful at this time: Lawrence O. Richards, *A New Face for the Church* (Grand Rapids: Zondervan, 1970), and Dietrich Bonhoeffer, *Life Together* (New York: Harper & Row, 1954).
[2]Alexander Roberts and James Donaldson, ed., *The Ante-Nicene Fathers* (Grand Rapids: Eerdmans, 1979), vol. 5, p. 425.

Chapter 1
[1]Charles Templeton, *Act of God* (Toronto: Seal Books, McClelland and Stewart-Bantam Limited, 1977).
[2]Howard A. Snyder, *The Community of the King* (Downers Grove, Ill.; InterVarsity Press, 1977), p. 119.
[3]Hans Küng, *The Church* (New York: Sheed and Ward, 1967), p. 97.
[4]David Watson, *I Believe in the Church* (London: Hodder & Stoughton, 1978), p. 18.
[5]J. I. Packer, "Renewal and Revival," *Renewal* (April-May, 1976), 62:14-17.
[6]Elisabeth Elliot, *Let Me Be a Woman* (Wheaton, Ill.: Tyndale, 1976), p. 42.
[7]Charles Swindoll, *Strike the Original Match* (Portland, Ore.: Multnomah Press, 1980), p. 10.

Chapter 2
[1]C. F. Keil and F. Delitzsch, *Biblical Commentary on the Old Testament: The Twelve Minor Prophets,* 8th ed. (Grand Rapids: Eerdmans, 1971), p. 428.
[2]Joyce G. Baldwin, *Haggai, Zechariah, Malachi: An Introduction and Commentary* (Downers Grove, Ill.: InterVarsity Press, 1972), pp. 221-22.
[3]Ibid., p. 222.
[4]T. Miles Bennett, *The Broadman Bible Commentary* (Nashville: Broadman Press, 1972), vol. 7, pp. 374-75.
[5]Arthur Wallis, *God's Chosen Fast* (London: Victory Press, 1958), p. 29.
[6]A helpful starter for those who are inexperienced in this area is Richard J. Foster, *Celebration of Discipline* (New York: Harper & Row, 1978).
[7]G. W. Barrett and J. V. L. Casserly, eds., *Dialogue on Destiny* (Greenwich, Conn.: Seabury, 1955), p. 76.

Chapter 3

[1]Paul Waitman Hoon, *The Integrity of Worship: Ecumenical and Pastoral Studies in Liturgical Theology* (New York: Abingdon, 1971), p. 56.

[2]C. S. Lewis, *Reflections on the Psalms* (New York: Brace & World, 1958), pp. 94-95.

[3]Ibid., p. 95.

[4]Karen Mains, "How to Teach Children to Worship," *Moody Monthly* (July-August 1978) p. 39.

[5]Hoon, p. 58.

[6]John Wesley, *Plain Account of Christian Perfection* (London: Epworth Press, 1952), p. 88.

[7]Thomas Smail, *Reflected Glory: The Spirit in Christ and Christians* (London: Hodder & Stoughton, 1975), pp. 11-12.

[8]Hoon, p. 56.

[9]Dietrich Bonhoeffer, *Life Together* (New York: Harper & Row, 1954), p. 94.

[10]Tom Smail et al., "Gospel and Spirit: A Joint Statement," Theological Renewal Occasional Paper, No. 1 (Surrey: Fountain Trust, 1977), p. 6.

[11]David Watson, *I Believe in Evangelism* (Grand Rapids: Eerdmans, 1976, p. 173.

Chapter 4

[1]From "The Chicago Call: An Appeal to Evangelicals," in *The Orthodox Evangelicals,* ed. Robert Webber and Donald G. Bloesch, (Nashville and New York: Thomas Nelson, 1978), p. 12.

[2]Ibid., p. 14.

[3]Quotations of the Didache follow the translation found in *The Apostolic Fathers,* ed. Jack Sparks (New York: Thomas Nelson, 1978).

[4]F. F. Bruce, *1 and 2 Corinthians,* New Century Bible (London: Oliphants, 1971), pp. 111-12.

[5]Ralph P. Martin, *Worship in the Early Church* (Grand Rapids: Eerdmans, 1974), p. 126.

[6]Robert E. Webber, *Common Roots: An Evangelical Call to Maturity* (Grand Rapids: Zondervan, 1978), p. 100.

[7]William D. Maxwell, *An Outline of Christian Worship* (London: Oxford Univ. Press, 1936), p. 112.

[8]Thomas Howard, "A Call to Sacramental Integrity" in *The Orthodox Evangelicals,* pp. 124-25.

[9]Webber, *Common Roots,* p. 101.

[10]C. S. Lewis, *Reflections on the Psalms,* p. 93.

[11]Hoon, pp. 28, 59.

[12]Hoon, p. 28.

Chapter 5
[1]Thomas A. Smail, "Authentic Authority," *Theological Renewal* (February-March 1976), 2:4.
[2]T. W. Manson, *The Church's Ministry* (London: Hodder & Stoughton, 1948), p. 27.
[3]T. Paul Stevens, "The Price of Leadership," HIS magazine (January 1974), pp. 11-12, 16.
[4]Michael Harper, *Let My People Grow* (Plainfield, N.J.: Logos, 1977), p. 86.

Chapter 6
[1]Howard Hendricks, *Don't Fake It . . . Say It with Love* (Wheaton, Ill.: Victor Books, 1974), pp. 113-14.
[2]Howard A. Snyder, *The Community of the King* (Downers Grove, Ill.: InterVarsity Press, 1977), p. 86.
[3]William Hendricksen, *I-II Timothy and Titus,* New Testament Commentary (Grand Rapids: Baker, 1957), p. 121.
[4]Karen Burton Mains, *Open Heart, Open Home* (Elgin, Ill.: David C. Cook, 1976), p. 28.
[5]"Some have taken the last three words as applying to the children (cf. Moffatt's ' . . . keep his children submissive and perfectly respectful'), but the noun **dignity** (Gk. *semnotēs*) seems more appropriate to the father's attitude. The point is that he must maintain strict discipline, but without fuss or resort to violence," J. N. D. Kelly, *The Pastoral Epistles* (London: Adam and Charles Black, 1963), p. 78.

Chapter 7
[1]Paul Simon, "Fifty Ways to Leave Your Lover," from the album *Still Crazy after All These Years* (New York: Columbia Records, 1975).
[2]Quoted in André Bustanoby, "When Wedlock Becomes Deadlock: Part II," *Christianity Today* (July 18, 1975), p. 11.
[3]Judith S. Wallerstein and Joan B. Kelly, "California's Children of Divorce," *Psychology Today* (January 1980), pp. 67-76. "The Children of Divorce," *Newsweek* (February 11, 1980), pp. 58-66.
[4]Quoted in Guy Duty, *Divorce and Remarriage* (Minneapolis: Bethany Fellowship, 1967), pp. 34-35.
[5]John Murray, *Divorce* (Grand Rapids: Baker, 1972), pp. 9-10.
[6]Alfred Edersheim, *Sketches of Jewish Social Life* (Grand Rapids: Eerdmans, 1957), pp. 157-58.

[7]John R. W. Stott, *Divorce* (Downers Grove, Ill.: InterVarsity Press, 1973), pp. 18-20.

[8]Dwight Hervey Small, *Design for Christian Marriage* (New York: Pyramid Books, 1971), p. 10.

[9]Dwight Hervey Small, *The Right to Remarry* (Old Tappan, New Jersey: Fleming Revell, 1977), p. 182.

[10]A helpful handbook for such counseling is Robert and Alice Fryling, *A Handbook for Engaged Couples* (Downers Grove, Ill.: InterVarsity Press, 1977).

Chapter 8

[1]Ronald J. Sider, *Rich Christians in an Age of Hunger* (Downers Grove, Ill.: InterVarsity Press), 1977), pp. 98-112.

[2]Malcolm Muggeridge, *Christ and the Media* (Grand Rapids: Eerdmans, 1977), pp. 23-42.

[3]John White details this problem more completely in *The Golden Cow* (Downers Grove, Ill.: InterVarsity Press), 1979.

Chapter 9

[1]John Wesley, *The Works of the Reverend John Wesley* (New York: B. Waugh and T. Mason, 1835), vol. 7, p. 317.

[2]Stanley C. Balwin, "The Prosperity Fallacy," *Eternity* (October 1979), pp. 46-47.

[3]Ibid.

[4]Quoted in Elisabeth Elliot, *Let Me Be a Woman* (Wheaton: Tyndale, 1976), p. 153.

[5]Clyde Hoeldtke, *Interchange,* Newsletter of Step 2 Ministries, Summer 1977.

[6]For a revealing and compelling assemblage of biblical texts pertaining to hunger, justice and the poor, see *Cry Justice: The Bible Speaks on Hunger and Poverty,* ed. Ronald J. Sider (Downers Grove, Ill.: InterVarsity Press, 1980).

[7]Harold Kuhn, "On Being Critically Consistently Prophetic," *Christianity Today* (September 22, 1978), pp. 53-55.

[8]For example, Sider suggests on an income of $13,000 a family might decide to give ten per cent of the first $8,000, fifteen per cent of the next $1,000, twenty per cent of the next $1,000 and so on for a total of $2,050 ($750 more than a straight ten per cent on $13,000). For further details see *The Graduated Tithe* (Downers Grove, Ill.: InterVarsity Press, 1978).

[9]Ronald J. Sider, *Rich Christians in an Age of Hunger* (Downers Grove,

Ill.: InterVarsity Press, 1977), p. 111.
[10]Wally Kroeker, "Enough," *Moody Monthly* (May 1975), p. 24.
[11]Ibid., p. 24.
[12]Peter Davids, "Wealth and the People of God," *Latin American Evangelist* (March-April 1976), p. 3.

Chapter 10

[1]From a booklet given to visitors of the Evangelical Sisterhood of Mary in Darmstadt, describing the ministry of the sisterhood.

[2]Although many of the prophecies given through the charismatic movement appear to be banal and predictable, there are some which even noncharismatics should want to heed. One such prophecy was given by Fr. Michael Scanlan at a meeting of the National Service Committee of the Catholic Charismatic Renewal (USA):

"The Lord God says, Hear my word:

"The time that has been marked by my blessing and gifts is being replaced now by the period to be marked by my judgment and purification. What I have not accomplished by blessings and gifts, I will accomplish by judgment and purification.

"My people, my church, is desperately in need of this judgment. They have continued in an adulterous relationship with the spirit of the world. They are not only infected with sin, but they teach sin, embrace sin, dismiss sin. Their leadership has been unable to handle this. There is fragmentation, confusion, throughout the ranks. Satan goes where he will and infects whom he will. He has free access throughout my people—and I will not stand for this.

"My people specially blessed in this renewal are more under the spirit of the world than they are under the Spirit of my baptism. They are more determined by fear of what others will think of them—fears of failure and rejection in the world, loss of respect of neighbors and superiors and those around them—than they are determined by fear of me and fear of infidelity to my word.

"Therefore your situation is very, very weak. Your power is so limited. You cannot be considered at this point in the center of the battle and the conflict that is going on.

"So this time is now come upon all of you: a time of judgment and of purification. Sin will be called sin. Satan will be unmasked. Fidelity will be held up for what it is and should be. My faithful servants will be seen and will come together. They will not be many in number. It will be a difficult and a necessary time. There will be collapse, difficulties, throughout the world.

"But more to the issue, there will be purification and persecution among my people. You will have to stand for what you believe. You will have to choose what word you will follow and whom you will respect.

"And in that choice, what has not been accomplished by the time of blessing and gifts will be accomplished. What has not been accomplished in the baptism and the flooding of gifts of my Spirit will be accomplished in a baptism of fire. The fire will move among you individually, corporately, in groups, and around the world.

"I will not tolerate the situation that is going on. I will not tolerate the mixture and the adulterous treating of gifts and graces and blessings with infidelity, sin, and prostitution. My time is now among you.

"What you need to do is to come before me in total submission to my word, in total submission to my plan, in total submission in this new hour. What you need to do is to drop those things that are your own, those things of the past. What you need to do is to see yourselves and those whom you have responsibility for in light of this hour of judgment and purification. You need to see them in that way and do for them what will best help them to stand strong and be among my faithful servants.

"For there will be casualties. It will not be easy, but it is necessary. It is necessary that my people be, in fact, my people; that my church be, in fact, my church; and that my Spirit, in fact, bring forth the purity of life, the purity and fidelity to the gospel." Quoted from Kevin and Dorothy Ranaghan, "God's Warning, God's Remedy," *The New Covenant* (May 1980), pp. 15-16.

[3]David Pawson, *Truth to Tell* (London: Hodder & Stoughton, 1977), p. 120.

[4]Eduard Schweizer, "πνεῦμα, πνευματικός," *Theological Dictionary of the New Testament,* VI, ed. Gerhard Friedrich (Grand Rapids: Eerdmans, 1967), p. 396.

[5]F. F. Bruce, *The Book of Acts,* The New International Commentary on the New Testament (Grand Rapids: Eerdmans, 1954), p. 84.

[6]James D. G. Dunn, *Baptism in the Holy Spirit* (London: SCM Press, 1970), p. 40.

[7]Thomas Smail, *Reflected Glory: The Spirit in Christ and Christians* (London: Hodder & Stoughton, 1975), pp. 40, 43, 141; Leon Joseph Suenens, *A New Pentecost?* (New York: Seabury, 1975), pp. 82, 84, 100; Larry Christenson, *The Charismatic Renewal among Lutherans* (Minneapolis: Lutheran Charismatic Renewal Services, 1976), pp. 37, 48, 99.

[8]Clark Pinnock, "The New Pentecostalism: Reflections of an Observer," *Perspectives on the New Pentecostalism,* ed. Russell P. Spittler (Grand

Rapids: Baker, 1976), p. 4.
[9]Smail, *Reflected Glory,* p. 153.
[10]Dennis J. Bennett, *Nine O'Clock in the Morning* (Plainfield, N.J.: Logos, 1970).
[11]Richard F. Lovelace, *Dynamics of Spiritual Life* (Downers Grove Ill.: InterVarsity Press, 1979), p. 125.
[12]Charles E. Hummel, *Fire in the Fireplace* (Downers Grove, Ill.: Inter-Varsity Press, 1978), p. 77.

Chapter 11
[1]Quoted in Philip Yancey, *Where Is God When It Hurts?* (Grand Rapids: Zondervan, 1977), p. 157.
[2]Georg Bertram, "παιδεύω," *Theological Dictionary of the New Testament,* V, ed. Gerhard Friedrich (Grand Rapids: Eerdmans, 1967), p. 618.
[3]Elisabeth Elliot Leitch, "The Glory of God's Will," in *Declare His Glory Among the Nations,* ed. David M. Howard (Downers Grove, Ill.: Inter-Varsity Press, 1977), p. 139.
[4]Cyril C. Richardson, *Early Christian Fathers* (Philadelphia: Westminster, 1953), vol. 1, p. 176.